Thomas Jefferson's
ROTUNDA
RESTORED

1973-76

A Pictorial Review
with Commentary

Frontispiece. The restored Rotunda, December 1976.

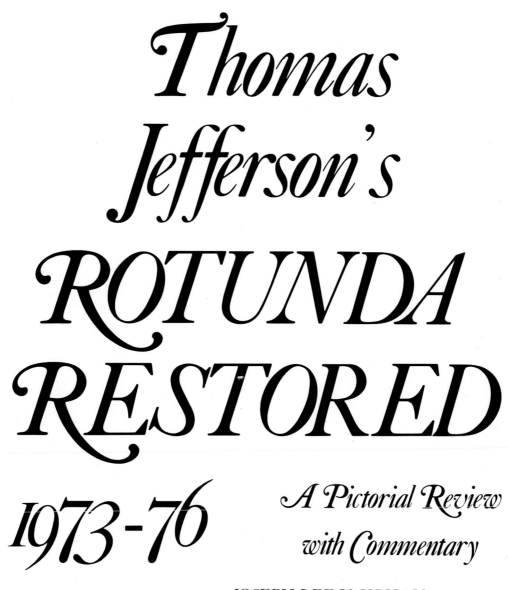

Thomas Jefferson's ROTUNDA RESTORED

1973-76

A Pictorial Review with Commentary

JOSEPH LEE VAUGHAN AND

OMER ALLAN GIANNINY, JR.

with a foreword by FREDERICK DOVETON NICHOLS

UNIVERSITY PRESS OF VIRGINIA   CHARLOTTESVILLE

This volume is published with the support of the
Thomas Jefferson Memorial Foundation

THE UNIVERSITY PRESS OF VIRGINIA
Copyright © 1981 by The Thomas Jefferson Memorial Foundation

First published in 1981

Library of Congress Cataloging in Publication Data

Vaughan, Joseph Lee.
  Thomas Jefferson's Rotunda restored, 1973–76.

  Bibliography: p.
  Includes index.
  1. Virginia. University. Rotunda—Conservation and
restoration.   2. Jefferson, Thomas, Pres. U. S., 1743–
1826.   I. Gianniny, Omer Allan, Jr., joint author.
II. Title.
LD5680.R87V38   378.755′482   80-27087
ISBN 0-8139-0888-4

Printed in the United States of America

*This book is dedicated to
Ann and Jean, often our most
penetrating critics and always
our most loving and loyal
supporters*

Contents

Illustrations

Illustrations

Illustrations

xi

Foreword

Thomas Jefferson's Rotunda Restored, 1973–76 *is the first book (probably of many) to be written about the return of Jefferson's famous academic building to much of its original form and function. The three Rotundas produced by modifications over the years are described in laymans' language rather than in architectural or construction terms, and color photographs of the restoration work done during 1973–76 and of the dedication ceremonies on April 13, 1976, are also included.*

Being Father of the University of Virginia was the occupation Jefferson chose for his final years. At the age of seventy-four, when most men today would be long retired, Jefferson embarked upon the great project of his old age. He not only laid out the curriculum, which was extremely advanced for his day, but he also selected all the books for the library, selected the professors, designed all the buildings, supervised their construction, and perhaps most important of all, coaxed a large sum of money, about a quarter of a million dollars, from a parsimonious and indifferent legislature. He knew that, once the university had opened, the politicians probably would never grant the final $55,000 needed to build the Rotunda, so he would not permit the university to open, even though all the other buildings were completed, until he had received the money for that building.

This splendid building was begun in 1823 and was completed the year Jefferson died, in 1826. It is said that in April of that year he spent several hours sitting in the Dome Room of the Rotunda, looking down the Lawn toward the vista of distant mountains, watching one of the final capitals being put in place and supervising some details of the bookcases being completed. When he left that afternoon for Monticello, he was never to return, but he had the satisfaction of knowing that his beloved university had opened in March of the preceding year and that with the completion of the Rotunda, he need have no more fears for its future.

Based on his conception of education and its future in the

United States, Jefferson planned a system of education that has largely been realized today. First of all, there would be elementary education: reading, writing, and arithmetic for all students—all children. The next level would be intermediate school, conforming to our high school, which would be for the training of technicians. Finally, for the professionals, there would be the university, which would train students of the highest intellectual caliber and achievements. The university was the capstone of education in the state, and the capstone of the architectural complex at the university was to be the rotunda. Upon it he lavished all of his skill and knowledge, and it is most fitting that in 1976, on the anniversary of the bicentennial of the American Declaration of Independence, the American Institute of Architects chose the University's buildings as the greatest complex of buildings erected in American since 1776.

Jefferson tells us that when he was in Paris as our minister—or in today's terms, our ambassador—from 1784 to 1789, he used every spare moment to study contemporary French architecture. At that time all of Europe was going to France to study the arts, and this movement might be called the first modern school of Paris, when aesthetics was uppermost in the minds of the Parisians. There was a series of great architects who were making experiments in large social complexes, who were concerned with the richness and variety of the ancient world, and who, finally, believed in the natural order of things. As geometry was, to them, one of the natural sciences, pure geometric shapes formed a large part of the theories of these men. Jefferson went out of his way to know the leading architects, some of whom he invited to dine at the beautiful American embassy on the Ronde Point on the Champs Elysées. When he came home, therefore, he was thoroughly trained as an architect through his vast study of European architectural and building styles. It was he who introduced French visionary architecture to North America, and today the Rotunda—embodying in its finished form all the ideas of that group—stands as the supreme example of that style in this country.

Although the burning of the Rotunda in 1895 was a tragic loss and seriously disrupted the community for some time, there were some gains. Until the fire, few people knew the university or Jefferson's brilliance as its architect, because it was remote from the centers of art and culture in nineteenth-century America. Reconstruction of the Rotunda following that fire, and the building of Cabell, Cocke, and Rouss halls by the distinguished firm of McKim, Mead & White also brought national attention. The fire set in motion a series of events that attracted gifts, support, and publicity, enhancing the university's reputation and raising expectations for its role in the twentieth century. Even as late as the 1950s, however, many people thought Stanford White had restored Jefferson's Rotunda. It is almost amusing to recall that when the restoration was mentioned on one occasion, a leading Virginia architect shook his head in disbelief and said: "It has always been my understanding that the Rotunda as rebuilt by Stanford White was exactly what Jefferson had planned."

In this book the facts surrounding the decisions to alter the Rotunda following the fire are detailed with documentation from minutes of the Board of Visitors, minutes of the faculty, and personal letters of participants. Though there was considerable controversy at the time, the Board of Visitors overrode opposition by faculty and alumni who wished to restore the Rotunda to the original form, and they approved White's plans, which removed the Dome Room to make space for an enlarged library. From 1898 to 1938, the Rotunda was the repository of the university's principal collections and served as the central undergraduate library.

Jefferson would never have agreed with White's plan to remove the Dome Room because for him it served as a symbol of the best in Western culture, and he insisted that its dimensions be exactly one-half those of the Pantheon, preserving its precise proportions. To Jefferson, it was a building that had endured for two thousand years and had been highly admired, and with such human admiration over so long a time, he believed a new Republic could not do better than to use it as the source of his design.

When White changed the building, he appears to have acted without the participation of his partner Charles F. McKim, a great classical expert and the man who had made the firm of McKim, Mead & White famous. McKim seems to have had no hand in the planning of the expanded university and apparently never visited the site. Yet it was he who had been responsible for the great buildings of the firm: the J.P. Morgan Library, the University Club, and Pennsylvania Station in New York and the Boston Public Library. White seems to have been primarily a New York socialite who obtained commissions and who was responsible for many country homes. He was responsible for more liberal interpretations of Renaissance design, including Madison Square Garden (where he was murdered) and the Metropolitan Club in New York.

In addition to the changes in the Rotunda, White proposed three new buildings to replace the ugly Annex on the north side of the Rotunda, which the faculty and Board of Visitors had decided not to rebuild. Cabell Hall was placed in the location that closed the vista to the distant mountains. It was flanked by Cocke and Rouss halls, containing additional lecture and laboratory rooms. The auditorium was located in the back of Cabell Hall. This group constituted a design error that Jefferson, and probably McKim, would never have been a party to. Though White made a weak recommendation for an alternate site, he readily accepted the board's preference for the site finally chosen.

The original design of the Lawn was expressly created to symbolize Jefferson's ideas of education—which would train and encourage the limitless freedoms of the human mind. Jefferson used falling terraces, as they were called, to lead the eye of the spectator from the Rotunda to the view of the mountains. He also used another Renaissance and Mannerist trick to increase the apparent length of the Lawn by making the pavilions farther apart as they were placed away from the Rotunda; this gave a false perspective that also increased the visual length and the architectural importance of the Lawn. It was also an error for White to create a view from the Rotunda that made Cabell Hall look as if it were rising out of the ground because one cannot see the basement level or the steps. From all these points of view, the closing of the Lawn was a mistake almost as serious as that of obliterating Jefferson's carefully designed interior of the Rotunda.

Because he considered it aesthetically important, Jefferson mentioned several times that the Rotunda was based on the Pantheon at one-half scale, both in its interior and its exterior dimensions. Fortunately, he had a sloping site, so he could obtain his utilitarian classrooms by raising the building on its foundation. The building was a pure geometric shape. The top of the dome formed the top of the sphere, the base of which was on the ground, or basement, level.

There are some three thousand documents in the Alderman Library to illustrate the history of the original building by Jefferson. These include not only his drawings of the building and specifications but also bills, estimates, letters to workmen, letters of recommendation concerning workmen, and various letters describing the work on the buildings as well as their symbolic importance. In his own words, "the great object of our aim from the beginning has been to make the establishment the most eminent in the United States. . . . We have proposed therefore to call to it characters of the first order of science from Europe . . . but by the distinguished scale of its structure and preparation . . . to induce them to commit their reputations to it. . . . To stop where we are is to abandon our high hopes, and become suitors to Yale and Harvard for their secondary characters."[1] This attention to aesthetics gives us

1. Thomas Jefferson, Monticello, December 28, 1822, to Joseph C. Cabell, Jefferson Papers, Library of Congress, quoted in *Early History of the University of Virginia as Contained in the Letters of Thomas Jefferson and Joseph C. Cabell* (Richmond: J. W. Randolph, 1856), pp. 260–61.

some idea of the good reasons for Jefferson's great care in the design of the buildings. Certainly the award from the American Institute of Architects in 1976 emphasized that his attention and care had been worth the effort.

The care that Jefferson lavished upon his masterpiece was responsible for the desire of the University to restore the building in the twentieth century. It should be pointed out that in this book the word restoration *is used in its true and accurate meaning in relation to architecture according to the Oxford English Dictionary:* Restoration *means "the process of carrying out alterations and repairs with the idea of restoring a building to something like its original form; a general renovation."² Great care was taken to assure the accuracy of the restoration. It was necessary to research three-thousand of the drawings, photographs, letters, and bills, including the proctor's papers. About a year was spent documenting the original design.*

Thus, the restoration is correct to the smallest detail. Like all modern museums of early American art and architecture, the building is fitted with heat, air conditioning, electricity, security and fire devices, and plumbing. Even Monticello, which is highly regarded as a carefully restored early building—and fortunately with most of its original furnishings—has those modern services.

Jefferson's original design for the interior, including the superb Dome Room, cannot be overestimated as a physical embodiment of his love of education and of books. By reflecting Palladio, one of those who had drawn the masterpieces of the ancient world, he was giving to the new world what he

---

2. Different uses of the term *restoration* were evident in the 1896–98 period, when Stanford White rebuilt the Rotunda following the great fire of 1895. At that time, many people spoke of restoring the university, which had been so largely damaged by the fire. The press applied the term to the reconstruction of the Rotunda. In 1939–40, the term was used once again in conjunction with Rotunda renovation, but the repairs at that time were relatively minor. Neither occasion led to an attempt to return the building to its original form.

thought was unrivaled architectural space, a space that would properly house his beloved books. He believed with all his heart that an educated man would always be a free man who would never allow himself to become a slave. It was fitting that the room that marked the capstone of the university housed those books that in Jefferson's opinion would guarantee the eternal freedom of the American people.

FREDERICK D. NICHOLS

Acknowledgments

Many people have helped us to prepare this book. Their enthusiasm and expertise have contributed to the substance and spirit of the enterprise. While the full responsibility for the content rests with the authors, in a real sense this book represents a community of effort. Those who have participated include the following:

Frederick D. Nichols expressed his continuing interest in this project in very concrete ways, as a reviewer of many of the slides and by using a selection of them in his lectures in 1977 and 1978. He also joined us for a tape-recorded interview on the restoration on May 11, 1978, and he read this manuscript in draft form, supplying professional information on research and design decisions reached during the planning for restoration.

Edgar F. Shannon, Jr., president of the University from 1959 until 1974, joined us for a personal interview on his role in the restoration on June 15, 1979.

Francis L. Berkeley, Jr., suggested that the record be kept photographically. He shared with us his chronology of the restoration and of the Rotunda's history and joined us for a personal interview on his role in the restoration on April 20, 1978.

Raymond C. Bice, Jr., joined us for an interview on April 18, 1978, encouraged our work, and made suggestions for substantive inclusion and for persons who might assist.

Joseph Headstream made comments and suggestions during construction.

John Herring showed some of the photographs in Newcomb Hall Gallery, 1977.

The University Guide Service sponsored a series of presentations during the spring of 1977 to guides and to the general public utilizing our slides.

Luther Y. Gore assisted by keeping up the continuity of photographing while Vaughan and Gianniny were away from the university.

Priscilla Critzer typed the rough manuscript and transcribed interview tapes.

T. Graham Hereford and John L. Longley, Jr., read the text.

Michael F. Plunkett and his associates in Alderman Library's Manuscripts Division helped locate, copy, and arrange permission for use of historic black and white photographs.

The University of Virginia Alumni Association underwrote the cost of film and processing, and distributed two copies of slide presentations on restoration. Gilbert J. Sullivan, Clay E. DeLauney, and Angus Macaulay were especially helpful.

Architect Louis W. Ballou was in frequent contact with Joseph L. Vaughan, both as a friend and as

Acknowledgments

an advisor, during the construction period. He also reviewed the slide collection and used several slides in an oral report to the United States Department of Housing and Urban Development. He joined us for an interview on the restoration on February 16, 1978.

Contractor Robert E. "Bobby" Lee reviewed our slides and engaged us to prepare a report to the Associated General Contractors of America, Inc., in 1976–77.

R. E. "Robin" Lee, Jr., and J. A. "Buddy" Kessler, Jr., reviewed the text and photographs in that report and, in so doing, shared their knowledge of the work. Mr. Kessler joined us for an interview on October 12, 1978.

Fred Warner, General Superintendent, reviewed all of the slide collection and tape-recorded a commentary on the work as seen in the slides.

Schuyler Reed, Associate General Superintendent, offered helpful observations and comments during construction, often directing photographers to interesting points related to work in progress.

Many craftsmen who worked on the Rotunda shared their perceptions and ideas with us.

The Albemarle Art Association invited us initially in December 1976 to show the slides to their members. Mrs. T. L. W. Bailey, president, was especially helpful and gracious.

Mrs. Alease Powley and Mrs. Ruby Raines typed drafts of the manuscript.

The Board of Directors of the Thomas Jefferson Memorial Foundation generously agreed to underwrite the cost of publishing this book, and the foundation's committee on research publication suggested that we expand the scope of what had begun as a pictorial review of the work of restoration to include more material of interest to preservation and restoration groups.

JOSEPH L. VAUGHAN
O. ALLAN GIANNINY, JR.

Introduction

E. WATTS,
BOOK-BINDER,
CHARLOTTESVILLE,
VIRGINIA.

Here was buried
Thomas Jefferson
Author of the Declaration of American Independence
of the Statute of Virginia for religious freedom
& Father of the University of Virginia.

Thomas Jefferson's epitaph,
written by him with the instruction
that the inscription should contain
"not a word more."

Introduction

When Thomas Jefferson penned his epitaph, stating that he was Father of the University of Virginia, he was referring to an historic fact and to a sense of commitment to the institution that had grown to be his dominant concern during the last decade of his life. As Father of the University of Virginia, he was personally in control of the academic program, the administrative structure, the location and design of buildings—all of which combined to form the "academical village."

This small university, often described as the first architecturally planned campus in America, was located in a rural region of Albemarle County, Virginia, seventy miles northwest from Richmond and a little over one hundred miles southwest from Washington, D.C. It was approximately one mile in the country from the small town of Charlottesville and was erected under the direct supervision of Thomas Jefferson between the years 1817 and 1826. Jefferson thought of the University of Virginia as a model for a new American style of higher education, with roots in the finest human traditions of the classical world and with its program of studies directed towards the sciences and disciplines most suitable for the future leaders of the state and the nation. Jefferson's concept of the university included a style of architecture that constantly reminded students and faculty alike of the classical roots of Western civilization. The buildings were arranged in rows of dormitories punctuated by pavilions, in which the professors lived and conducted their classes. At the highest point of ground, and in the closed north end of the area, was placed the Rotunda, the architectural and academic center of the university. The dome of this building, modeled after the Pantheon of Rome, became familiar the world over. The building has come to symbolize American higher education, so that its influence has extended far beyond the little group of red-brick buildings erected in the Virginia countryside in the early nineteenth century.

After completion of the university, the Rotunda underwent changes in 1850 as the massive Annex was added under the direction of Robert Mills. In 1896–98 the building was reconstructed following a devastating fire that destroyed the Annex and gutted the Rotunda. That reconstruction, under the direction of Stanford White, included major alterations of the interior to enlarge the university's library. In 1938 the library was moved to another building, and in the years 1973 to 1976 the Rotunda was modified once again to return it to its original structural appearance. We were witnesses when the building revealed its secrets of a century-and-a-half of history, which had included destruction by fire, remodeling, maintenance and repair, use, and even neglect. Architect and builder, construction superintendent, and many workers helped us see and record photographically what might interest experts and laymen at a later time. Many of those features and much of the reconstruction are now buried once again under twelve feet of Albemarle County clay.

This book is divided into two parts. In Part I, we

review something of the building's history leading up to the most recent work of restoration and adaptation. In Part II, we present a photographic story in color of the 1973–76 restoration.

The book is essentially a chronology of the Rotunda, showing the major developments at the several stages of its modification, both in its functions within the university and in its structure. At the end of Part I and as a transition to Part II, there is a general discussion of the problems of restoration that were raised and that affected the decisions related to the recent restoration. Without making judgments as to how frequently these particular problems and issues are encountered by persons engaged in preservation and restoration work in other places, it has seemed appropriate to describe them as a part of this record.

It is our view that in the history of this building we can see those general issues of preservation and restoration that occur when any famous and important building is to be preserved or restored. Questions about adhering to the original concept must be balanced by the restorers against the need to adapt the building to meet new uses and conditions. As we shall show, that pairing of concerns has been present throughout the entire history of this building.

In addition to the three major versions of the Rotunda—by Jefferson, by White, and the most recent one under the direction of Architect Louis W. Ballou of the firm of Ballou and Justice, Richmond, Virginia—there were two other occasions when the building underwent relatively minor changes. During the 1870s, largely to protect the building from leakage through the roof, repairs and modifications were made to the dome. The stepped rings installed by Jefferson were removed, and the roof took on a severely curved, spherical form. At the same time, a small cupola was added above the skylight to prevent water leakage through that opening. Actually, cupolas similar to the one shown in figure 6 seem to have been added and removed several times during the nineteenth century in attempts to stop leakage. The second modification occurred in 1939 and 1940, when the building was refurbished after removal of the library to the new Alderman building. Most of this work was devoted to repairs of terrace wings and to the general overhaul of weather surfaces without change of obvious features, but it was called a restoration. We shall review those smaller modifications briefly in Part I.

The present account of reconstruction during the period from 1973 until 1976 was undertaken by us at the request of the chairman of the Restoration Committee to show a nontechnical view of the work. That remains the object of the book. It became clear in preparation of the pictorial story, however, that some history of the building would be necessary to give a context for the photographic account, and the first part of this book is intended primarily to give that perspective.

Accounts of the original building have been detailed by others,[1] and there is no attempt to review those treatments here.

This book also differs from previous treatments of the building in presenting fleeting views of work in progress—when old structures were exposed briefly, only to be covered over by the next operation of the builder. In the pages that follow, Part I is the prologue to the photographic story in Part II.

1. William B. O'Neal, *Jefferson's Buildings at the University of Virginia: The Rotunda*, presents the story of the original construction under direction of Thomas Jefferson. Reconstruction of the building following the fire of 1895 is the subject of a book currently in progress by Frederick D. Nichols and O. Allan Gianniny, Jr.

I

Background

UNIVERSITY OF VIRGINIA

From the East

They have nearly finished the Rotunda. The pillars of the Portico are completed and it greatly improves the appearance of the whole—The books are removed into the Library—and we have a very fine collection.

Edgar Allan Poe to John Allan, from the university, September 21, 1826.

Jefferson's Concept of the Rotunda

*T*homas Jefferson's efforts as a statesman overshadowed his work as an architect. Though his contemporaries were well aware of his abilities as an architect, subsequent generations failed to credit those abilities until Fiske Kimball published *Thomas Jefferson, Architect*, in 1916.[1] Kimball noted that Jefferson's work on the University of Virginia had led others to invite him to design buildings for them. Later, however, Jefferson's biographers gave "more and more fleeting mention" of his architectural work. In Kimball's view, the nineteenth-century biographers could not accept the idea that a man in public life might take artistic interests seriously, though he might indulge in them during his hours of relaxation.[2]

Kimball also rejected the claims of architectural

---

1. Fiske Kimball, *Thomas Jefferson, Architect* (Boston: Printed for Private Distribution at the Riverside Press, Cambridge, Mass., 1916; republished unabridged and with a new introduction by Frederick Doveton Nichols, New York: Da Capo Press, 1968). The title page describes the book as presenting: "Original designs in the collection of Thomas Jefferson Coolidge, Junior with an essay and notes by Fiske Kimball."

2. Ibid., pp. 80–81, 14–15.

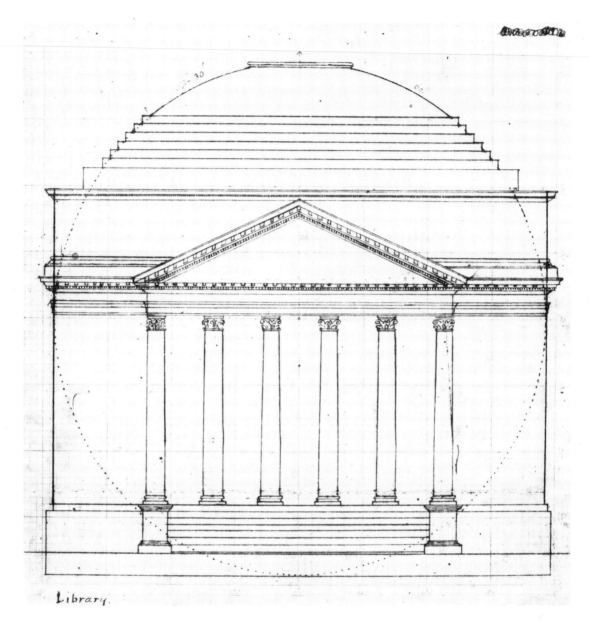

Library.

1. Rotunda elevation (ca. 1819–21), entitled "Library"
(N 328).

> *"Having received from all our brethren approbations on the loan, I authorised Mr. [Arthur S.] Brockenbrough [proctor of the university] to engage the work of the Rotunda, and have it commenced immediately."*
>
> (Thomas Jefferson to Board of Visitors, March 12, 1823. Entry 1984, Jefferson Papers, University of Virginia, quoted in O'Neal, *Jefferson's Buildings at the University of Virginia: The Rotunda*, p. 25.)

critics of the early twentieth century who gave credit
for the design of the university to professional architects
who had advised Jefferson on the layout of the university and the design of its buildings. William Thornton,
Benjamin H. Latrobe, and Robert Mills had been
named by some critics as persons to whom credit should
go, but Kimball pointed out that these and others of
Jefferson's contemporaries acknowledged that the general architectural conception of the university belonged
to Jefferson.

Avoiding extravagant claims, but allowing the Jefferson drawings to demonstrate his point, Kimball
believed he had restored Jefferson's reputation as a
major contributor to American architecture.

Jefferson's drawings of the university, including
those of the Rotunda (fig. 1, 2, 3, 4), were cited by
Kimball, though they were not reproduced in his book.[3]
The first comprehensive account of Jefferson's work in
designing and supervising construction of the Rotunda
was published by O'Neal in 1960.[4]

O'Neal recounts that in 1817, when replying to
Jefferson's request for suggestions on the layout of the
university and the design of its buildings, Latrobe recommended that a domed building be placed at the
center of the university. Latrobe proposed that the

3. Kimball's object was to demonstrate the range of Jefferson's architectural work by publishing a collection of drawings that had been unavailable to scholars or to the public. The drawings of the university had
already been published in Herbert B. Adams, *Thomas Jefferson and the University of Virginia* (U.S. Bureau of Education circular of information no. 2
[Washington, D.C.: U.S. Government Printing Office, 1888]), so they
were available to Kimball's readers.

4. William B. O'Neal, *Jefferson's Buildings at the University of Virginia:
The Rotunda*. O'Neal presented a narrative account of the design and construction of the Rotunda from 1817 until Jefferson's death on July 4, 1826.
Excerpts from supporting documents, letters, and drawings follow the
work until 1828, when construction was substantially completed.

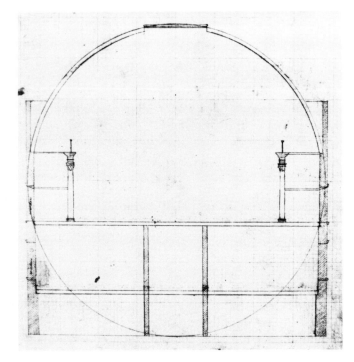

2. Rotunda, vertical section, (ca. 1819–21) (N 329).

"The ROTUNDA . . . is 77 feet in diameter, and in height, crowned by a Dome 120 deg. of the sphere. The lower floor has large rooms for religious worship, for public examinations, and other associated purposes. The upper floor is a single room for a library, canopied by the Dome and it's [sic] skylight."

(From "An explanation of the ground plan of the University of Virginia," prepared for sale to prospective students in 1825. Reprinted in Edwin M. Betts, "Groundplans and Prints of the University of Virginia," *Proceedings of the American Philosophical Society* 90, no. 2 [1946]:86.)

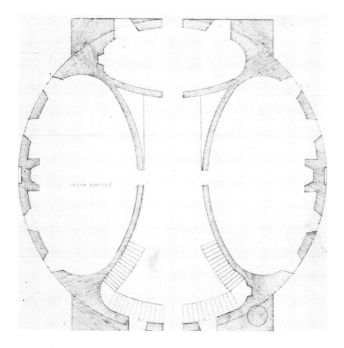

3. Rotunda, first-floor plan, as constructed in 1823
(N 330).

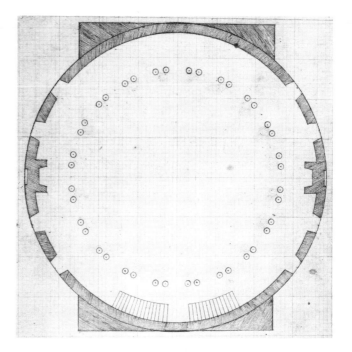

4. Rotunda, plan of the Dome Room, as constructed in
1823 (N 331).

building should "exhibit in mass details as perfect a specimen of architectural taste as can be devised." Following Jefferson's proposed uses for the building, he called for three floors, of which the upper would have a "circular room under the dome." Attached to the letter was a sketch showing a ground plan with a rectangular building at the center, but with a dome set on its top.[5]

Jefferson was quite familiar with domed buildings. His collected drawings show that he had studied them in France and England in 1784–89. He had built the octagonal dome at Monticello and had proposed small domes for other homes and buildings. He had also closely followed the work of William Thornton and Latrobe in the design and construction of the national capitol.

Although Jefferson selected the Pantheon of Rome as his model for the library of the university, he had never seen the Pantheon itself. He went, therefore, to the drawings of Andrea Palladio. He may even have gotten the name for his building from Palladio, who used the Christian name given to the Pantheon by Pope Boniface IV when it became a cathedral about 607 A.D.—the Santa Maria della Rotonda. Both Thornton and Latrobe acknowledged that the final design was exclusively the work of Jefferson.

Jefferson reduced the diameter of the Pantheon by half for his own building, to balance the architectural grandeur of the original with the practical needs of an infant university being built with severely limited

5. Benjamin H. Latrobe, Washington, D.C., to T.J., July 24, 1817, Jefferson Papers, Library of Congress. This letter, quoted by O'Neal (p. 19), was one in a series of letters between Jefferson and Latrobe in the summer of 1817, discussing the layout and design of the university. Excerpts from this series also appear in Kimball, *Thomas Jefferson, Architect*, pp. 187–92.

funds. For the same reason, he used locally fired red brick in the Rotunda rather than the stone construction employed in the Pantheon. His decisions opened the way for his own innovations in design and reduced the technical problems of construction, especially in the supporting structure needed for the domed roof, which was fabricated from wooden timbers. Part of the innovation resulted from the necessity to use materials that could be obtained or manufactured locally. The bricks were made in kilns in the immediate vicinity, using local clay, and the lumber was cut from timber on the site. Exterior features were all of local materials, except that column capitals on the porticos were carved from Carrara marble and imported at great cost and difficulty. Inside the building, the columns were made of wood, and the capitals were carved of black locust.

The Dome Room—though inspired by the design of the Pantheon—was no mere copy. Jefferson had selected it to house the library of the university, departing from Latrobe's suggestion that it be a large meeting room. The main area of the room was surrounded by a ring of twenty pairs of columns that supported two balconies for the storage of books. Its scale and detail would differ enough from the Pantheon that it would reflect Jefferson's own idea of the room that was to be the functional center of the university as well as its architectural focal point. (See fig. 5.)

On the two floors below the Dome Room, Jefferson placed large oval rooms that could accommodate all the students and faculty for lectures. The building would give mass and detail that showed architectural taste, as Latrobe had suggested, but it also differed from his concept. Jefferson made the height of the building equal to its diameter, so that geometrically it amounted to a

5. Interior of the Dome Room before the fire of 1895.

"The use of the Library is freer and fuller now than ever before, perhaps, and this gratifying increase had made necessary additional furniture. This increasing use speaks well for the intellectual life of the University. . . . The greatest need is a fireproof library building. Our present valuable collection is constantly exposed to fire, and has, during this severe winter, suffered from water, on account of the melting of the heavy snowfall."

From an unsigned article, "The Library," *Alumni Bulletin of the University of Virginia*, O.S. 1 [1895]:109–10.

sphere set in a cylinder. The base of the sphere was at the level of the basement floor.

At the front, the Lawn was raised to reduce the apparent height of the building without disturbing its proportions. The effect was a smaller width and a greater height than the Pantheon, and Jefferson designed the portico to balance the new proportions. The portico was reached from the Lawn by fourteen steps, which lead the eye upward from the ground and give the building a light and lofty aspect.

Lower oval rooms in the main Rotunda were multipurpose. Each of the two lower floors had three oval rooms surrounding a free-form central hall, the first of its kind in America. As with the Dome Room, these lower floors represented a daring step for American architecture, bringing the concept of monumental European structures into an American university. All of Jefferson's long experience in architecture was brought to bear on this, his final and his greatest building. He felt great pleasure in showing the Rotunda to his European friends. For example, on November 15, 1824, he and James Madison were dinner hosts to the marquis de Lafayette in the uncompleted Dome Room.

He was justly proud of this building, both for its architecture and as a symbol of a fresh new American approach to higher education. He hoped that the structure of the building and its surrounding pavilions and dormitories would represent the freedom from provincial prejudices and from the influence of religious denominations. Drawing on the classical traditions of Greece and Rome and on the best modern science, he was, always, trying to educate the future leaders of the state and nation by means of their surroundings as well as through the classes they would take in the university.

The Annex and Other Buildings Added before 1895

*W*ithin a quarter century after the university was built, the number of students had grown, as had the needs of the university for additional space to house classrooms and laboratories. These demands led to the construction of a building, called the Annex, on the north side of the Rotunda. The Annex was constructed under the supervision of Robert Mills, the noted native-born American architect who was a protégé of Jefferson and was also trained by Latrobe. In 1853, Mills described the project as follows:

> *The great increase of students in the University and the want of suitable rooms for their exercises, have caused the erection of a building in the rear of the Rotunda, 150 feet long including Porticoes, and 50 feet wide, which from the declivity of the ground, will afford 4 large lecture rooms, a large exhibition room and museum above, all accessible from the Rotunda, from which it is separated by a colonnaded space. The Northern front is ornamented by a similar Portico to that of the Rotunda, in which will be placed the Statue of Mr. Jefferson.*
>
> *The view from this Portico will be magnificent, from the stretch of country lying North and East and West, and*

terminated by the Blue ridge of mountains, a beautiful agricultural region watered by the Rivanna and its tributaries, and traversed by the Rail-road from Charlottesville to Staunton.[6]

The Annex was never popular, and from the beginning there was fear that the connecting wooden roof would increase the danger of fire to the Rotunda.[7] The Annex was opened in 1853, and together with the Rotunda, it formed an expanded center for the activities of the university. At about this same time, the space under the terrace wings, formerly used as a gymnasium, had become inadequate for that purpose, and a wooden gymnasium had been erected at the foot of the Lawn, where the land dropped away steeply.[8]

From 1861 to 1865, during the Civil War, enrollment at the university fell to very low levels as all able-bodied students and faculty were called to the service of the Confederate States of America. The physical plant was not adequately maintained, so there was a great deal of deterioration during the war and the reconstruction period. At some time during the 1870s, there were minor modifications to improve the water-

6. Robert Mills, "Architecture in Virginia," *The Virginia Historical Register and Literary Companion* 6, no. 1 (1853):41.

7. The *Charlottesville Daily Progress* and the *Charlottesville Weekly Progress*, both dated Thursday, October 31, 1895, carried a description of architects' inspections of the burned buildings. This article also stated: "The father of Dr. W. C. N. Randolph, the rector, bitterly opposed the building of the Annex in 1852. He predicted that it would lead to the burning of the Rotunda." The reference is to Thomas Jefferson Randolph, grandson of Jefferson.

8. The location of this gymnasium appeared on a map of the grounds prepared by William A. Pratt, the university's first superintendent of buildings and grounds, about 1858. The map is in the university archives in Alderman Library and is reproduced in William B. O'Neal, *Pictorial History of the University of Virginia*, 2nd ed. (Charlottesville: University Press of Virginia, 1976), p. 59.

proof quality of the dome roof. When repairs were
made, the steps on the lower part of the dome, which
Jefferson had taken from the design of the Pantheon,
were removed, leaving a starkly curved line that was
unrelieved from the parapet to the skylight. As mentioned above, a cupola was erected on top of the skylight, apparently to make that opening watertight without sacrificing light in the Dome Room. (See fig. 6.)

Old photographs suggest that there may have been
other cupolas installed and removed during the nineteenth century. They seem to have had relatively short
lives. There were reports that the library collection
suffered from water leakage through the dome or the
skylight.[9] In each instance, the changes seem to have
been motivated more by the need for maintenance and
repair than by a desire to innovate in the design.

Other buildings were constructed at the university
after the Civil War, including the Brooks Museum,
completed in 1877, and the Miller Building, first used
as a chemistry laboratory and completed about 1869.
The Chapel was completed in 1890, and the Fayer-
weather Gymnasium in 1893. During the late 1880s
and early 1890s there was considerable growth in attendance at the university, and the faculty began to
look toward the expansion of facilities. Before any such
expansion could take place, however, a major fire destroyed the Annex completely and spread to the Rotunda, gutting its interior. This fire became the occasion
for planning and constructing a new set of buildings
that made a significant change in both the function and
the structure of the Rotunda, as it did for all of the
teaching facilities in the university.

9. "The Library," *The Alumni Bulletin of the University of Virginia,*
O.S.1(1895):109–10.

6. Rotunda exterior before the fire of 1895. The cupola
was added to prevent leakage around the skylight.

The Great Fire of 1895

*T*he fire occurred on Sunday, October 27, 1895, beginning in an upper storage room in the Annex and sweeping through both buildings within three to four hours after it was discovered (see fig. 7), and before firefighting equipment could be adequately marshaled from surrounding cities. A poignant and detailed description of the fire, not previously published, was written by John T. Thornton, son of William Mynn Thornton, chairman of the faculty. Young Thornton's mother was in Berlin, Germany, with two of his sisters and a younger brother who were studying there, and John was a student in the university. That Sunday evening, when his father was exhausted by the day's efforts, John wrote his mother to describe the shocking events of the day.

My dear mamma,

    I write to let you know of a most fearful calamity which has befallen the dear old University. This morning I heard cries of "fire" and found that the Annex was in flames. Everyone was running to the Rotunda and soon a large crowd

7. Rotunda burning, Sunday, October 27, 1895.

was assembled. No water could be gotten as high as the flames, only a miserable little stream of water about six feet in length came from the hose when at the level of the ground. In response to telegrams, Lynchburg and Richmond sent their engines by special trains, but the Lynchburg engine was delayed in the road and did not arrive within an hour of the expected time. I received a telegram from Richmond when the fire had been almost put out and wired back not to send the engine. There was nothing to do but to try to keep the fire from Buckmaster's and Tuttle's houses and to save all that was in the Rotunda and the Annex. They tried to blow up the Portico between the Annex and the Rotunda in the hope that, if the engine should arrive in time, the Rotunda might be saved, but all to no purpose. Soon the flames had gained possession of the Rotunda and nothing is now left standing but the base and the ruined walls. The boys worked like fiends to save all that was possible. Kent estimates that only one tenth of the books were saved but he is wrong—in my opinion at least one third or more were saved. The Austin collection was lost entirely. The statue of Jefferson, Minor's bust, the pictures were saved in fairly good condition. The School of Athens was lost. Uncle Frank's valuable physical apparatus was carried out but the greater part so broken as to be practically useless. Only 25,000 insurance wh[ich] nowhere near covers the loss. Is estimated th[at] 75,000 will scarcely rebuild the Rotunda and Annex to say nothing of the loss in books and instruments. No change in lectures which will continue as usual, the classes meeting in Wash[ington] Hall, Temperance Hall, Museum and professors' offices. Poppa is back in his old room—5 W[est] L[awn] where the Chairman's office will be. Poppa is so busy that he cannot write to you tonight and told me to let you know of the loss. Am so exhausted myself that I cannot write much. The professors are taking it bravely—not lamenting the past but making plans for the future. You can imagine how distressed everyone is. I myself, now that the excitement has worn off, am getting more and more miserable every minute and I cannot express to you my sorrow. I love this old University with all my heart, and I who am comparatively young, am so grieved what must be the distress of those old professors who have worked for the University so long and lectured so often within those now ruined walls! What a number of blows have struck the University in the year since you have been away! Misfortune after misfortune has crippled its usefulness and now that this crowning blow, this building planned and built by Jefferson, this splendid library, our so famous copy of the School of Athens, the dear old clock that never kept time, should be destroyed, seems to be the crowning evil and the worst that this nemesis who pursues us could let fall on our heads. Horrible! Horrible! Horrible! The thing gets worse the more I think about it. However lamentations do no good. We can only depend on State aid and the generosity of our alumni. Have just opened a telegram from George Anderson from Richmond saying he wanted to start a subscription immediately. Telegrams of sympathy come from all sides. O'Ferral seems especially interested. That is a good sign that the State will help us. Some taking a cheerful view of the situation say that in the end it will benefit the UVa by bringing her more before the people. Cannot offer any opinion on that subject. Thank you very much for the beautiful pair of gloves and more especially for thinking of me and my twentieth anniversary. Had intended to write you a special letter of thanks today but am too tired and miserable. Love to the children and yourself. Excuse hasty scribble and believe me. Your af. son.

John T. Thornton[10]

10. John T. Thornton to E. Rosalie Thornton, October 26 [27], 1895, Thornton Family Papers (accession no. 2077-c), Manuscripts Department, University of Virginia Library. "Kent" and "Uncle Frank," referred to by Thornton, were family members who were also members of the faculty. "Uncle Frank" was Francis H. Smith, professor of physics, whose wife was Mrs. Thornton's sister. "Kent" was Charles W. Kent, professor of English, whose wife was a daughter of the Smiths, and hence a niece of Mrs. Thornton. William Mynn Thornton, John's father, was professor of applied mathematics, director of instruction in engineering, and chairman of the faculty. This latter post was the highest administrative office in the university before the first president was installed in 1904. "Buckmaster" was Professor H. H. Buckmaster, a member of the medical faculty, and "Tuttle" was Albert H. Tuttle, professor of biology and agriculture. They lived in the pavilions next to the Rotunda, on East and West Lawn, respectively, and their houses were in danger of burning. The terrace wings connecting the Rotunda to these pavilions were intentionally blown up in an attempt to stop the spread of the fire. Actually, a change in direction of the wind is credited with the fire's burning itself out without destroying the buildings along the Lawn.

Accounts of the fire were published in the *Alumni Bulletin* O.S. 2:67–78; this issue, dated November 1895, was actually published in January 1896. Other accounts appeared in the newspapers—notably the *Charlottesville Chronicle*, the *Charlottesville Daily Progress*, and the *Richmond Dispatch*—beginning on Monday, October 28, 1895. The student newspaper, *College Topics*, reported on the fire and its aftermath in its next weekly edition, Saturday, November 2. A detailed account of the fire was also published by Morgan Portiaux Robinson, state archivist of Virginia, in *The Burning of the Rotunda* (Richmond: F. J. Mitchell, 1921).

8. Rotunda in ruins, Monday, October 28, 1895.

Plans
for Restoring the
University

*T*hornton's letter describes the fire in tones that were echoed by many persons over the next few days. The intense feeling of loss and the urgent sense that reconstruction must proceed immediately predominated in the university community. (See fig. 8.) On Sunday afternoon, even before the fire was fully extinguished, the faculty had met and had determined that classes must go on without interruption. Fearing that students might leave and fail to return, they acted quickly. They had also authorized the chairman to appoint a building committee to plan for restoration of the Rotunda and other necessary buildings as quickly as possible and to initiate efforts to raise the funds needed for that work. During the next week, the faculty's building committee met and reported to the faculty, first on Tuesday, October 29, for information, and then on Thursday, October 31, for action on their proposals for reconstruction. The *Richmond Dispatch*, the *Charlottesville Daily Progress*, and the *Charlottesville Chronicle* contained many reports during the week immediately following the fire

29

of efforts being made to restore or reconstruct the university.

On October 31, the faculty accepted a report from the building committee that proposed the restoration of the Rotunda to serve as an enlarged library. New buildings were proposed to house the academic departments of the university, to replace the large meeting hall destroyed with the Annex, and to house physics (natural philosophy), engineering, and law. They recommended that the Annex not be reconstructed, and that the new buildings be located instead at the foot of the Lawn. This proposal contained an ambiguous recommendation related to reconstruction of the Rotunda's interior. Sentiment was clearly in favor of rebuilding the Rotunda according to the Jefferson design, but the functional role of the building was now to be more specialized than ever. It was to be a library, and virtually all its other functions were to be removed to other locations in the university. The faculty action was explicit about the exterior of the building—decreeing that it be restored as closely as possible to the original lines of the Jefferson building as was consistent with fireproof construction. The entire interior was to be used as a library and to be readily accessible for that purpose from the portico floor up to the top of the dome. This latter statement would be the source of extensive controversy during the next four to five months.

On Friday, November 1, the *Charlottesville Chronicle* reported that the interior of the Rotunda "will be such that the building can be turned into a library." This statement was in contrast to a statement about the exterior: "The Rotunda will be constructed so as to appear, externally, just as it appeared before, except that it will have two porticoes." Viewed in retrospect, the story seems to imply that the interior would undergo some change.

On Monday, November 4, the Board of Visitors met in special session to hear the faculty proposals. They approved them in principle; appointed a committee for raising funds and a university building committee (which action, in effect, dismissed the faculty committee); and hired McDonald Brothers, Architects, of Louisville, Kentucky, to supervise reconstruction of the damaged terrace wings, to place a temporary cover over the ruins of the Rotunda, and to plan for its reconstruction.[11]

On Saturday, November 9, the student newspaper, *College Topics*, carried an editorial bitterly denouncing the decision of the faculty to convert the Rotunda to a library when that meant making a substantial change in the structure of the building. Somewhat facetiously they suggested that the change had been made to make the books happy and to keep them from feeling displaced. By contrast, the editorialist continued, the faculty and the Board of Visitors seem not to care that students were displaced. They recommended that the building be rebuilt to keep the same interior as the one

11. Harry P. McDonald, senior partner in the firm of McDonald Brothers, Architects, of Louisville, Kentucky, was in Charlottesville at the time of the fire, engaged in reconstruction of Christ Episcopal Church. He and his local associate, G. H. Spooner, an engineer, were invited to examine the ruins of the buildings, to determine the extent of the damages and report their estimates of the cost and time needed to rebuild the wings. They were also asked to advise how much of the remaining structure of the Rotunda could be used in reconstruction. Their first task was an emergency measure, undertaken in an attempt by the faculty to get desperately needed classrooms back into service as quickly as possible. McDonald Brothers was formally engaged by the Board of Visitors on November 4, to advise in the rebuilding of the Rotunda and the wings and in the demolishing of the ruins of the Annex.

before the fire and that functions of the building be made to fit its structure.

In the meantime, alumni and friends of the university had begun to raise funds and to encourage the university officials to restore the building as soon as possible. Newspaper headlines quoted alumni in Richmond as saying it must be rebuilt exactly as it was. Such statements did not always differentiate between Rotunda and Annex, however, and they said nothing about interior changes as compared to exterior shape. These distinctions were still only vaguely expressed by either the supporters or the news reporters. Details were overshadowed by the sense of urgency surrounding the reconstruction. Many people, including university officials, continued to fear that the university might lose its currently enrolled students and would surely fail to attract enough students for continued operation unless its facilities could be made usable at the earliest possible date. Officials set most unrealistic dates for completion of that work. For example, the *Charlottesville Daily Progress* had reported on October 31 that the walls of the Rotunda were satisfactory for use in rebuilding. They also quoted Harry P. McDonald as saying that the Rotunda and wings "can be rebuilt in such a short time that we refrain from stating it for fear that it may not be credited." In early November, the faculty members were speaking of the necessity for completing the rebuilding of the Rotunda in time for classes the following September; and McDonald's estimate had been that the wings could be returned to service by January 1896.

All of these statements underestimated the magnitude of the task of rebuilding; they clearly anticipated only a reconstruction of what had stood before. Even this expectation was at odds with the requirements that the faculty had considered essential in their first response to their own building committee—when they had voted without dissent that all new buildings erected to replace those destroyed must be fireproof, as must the reconstructed Rotunda and wings. This change required a redesign of the structure of interior floors and of the domed roof, selection and purchase of new materials, and erection of a new structure. Nevertheless, the faculty continued to talk of reopening the Rotunda by the fall of 1896.

Controversy over redesign of the Rotunda interior led to a special meeting of the faculty on November 20, 1895, when they attempted to remove ambiguity from their earlier report and to state categorically that the interior of the Rotunda should be restored to the same lines it had had before the fire. They passed a new resolution to be forwarded to the Board of Visitors.[12] But if the first resolution was ambiguous, the changes they wanted in the new building continued the confusion—improved lighting in the Dome Room (to be provided by an enlarged skylight), better heating, better ventilation, an option to the committee to remove a balcony, and a provision that the building be fireproof. Together these provisions conflicted with their recommendation, that the building be made to look like the old one. In addition, they left a number of decisions to the building committee and indicated the need for discretion and decisive action.

12. The minutes of the faculty meeting of November 20, 1895, appear in the university archives, including the report adopted at that meeting as well as some of the detailed discussion offered in support of a resolution that was passed and forwarded to the Executive Committee of the Board of Visitors.

They acknowledged that the report of October 31 had been ambiguous but insisted that it had been their intent to return the interior of the building to the design it had had before the fire. They forwarded their new resolution to the Executive Committee of the Board of Visitors for action.

Plans for reconstruction of the Rotunda were already underway under the direction of McDonald by the time the faculty reported their revised action. Only two days after the fire, McDonald had suggested that the Rotunda could be quickly reconstructed. The *Charlottesville Chronicle* reported that the terrace wings could be repaired for use as classrooms by the first of January 1896 and that the Rotunda itself could be rebuilt for use by the beginning of the fall session in September of 1896. McDonald, then employed as a consultant by the faculty building committee, had been engaged by the Board of Visitors on November 4, 1895, to "advise and assist in" reconstruction of the Rotunda and its wings. At the same time, the board had acted to approve a search for a nationally prominent architect to take charge of construction of the new buildings called for in the faculty report of October 31, 1895.

During November and December, McDonald and his Charlottesville associate, G. H. Spooner, supervised reconstruction of the terrace wings, substituting flat built-up roofs for the metal roofs over wooden rafters that had been on the original wings. In the course of this reconstruction, it became clear before the end of the year that McDonald's design for the new flat roofs lacked enough reinforcing steel, and the roofs began to crack and sag. Major changes would be needed in the design before these roofs could be completed. The wings would not be ready by January 1896 and would be considerably delayed: first, by the necessity for a redesign to correct the weakness; second, by an assignment of responsibility for the structural failures; and third, by the need for the university to decide what to do about the obvious incompetency shown in the design. On January 4, 1896, in the midst of this investigation, McDonald presented the building committee with a proposed design for the interior of the Rotunda (fig. 9). This showed the Rotunda open inside from portico floor to dome and presented an extremely elaborate interior of mixed orders of classical columns arranged in three tiers, one above the other and surrounding the central room.[13]

The building committee was preparing to select a nationally prominent architect to design new buildings and to prepare the landscape plan that included their location. A few days after the meeting on January 4, the members of the Building Committee determined to seek the withdrawal of McDonald from his assignment and to engage a single architect to plan and supervise all new construction, including the Rotunda. It had

13. By January 1896, McDonald had also supervised the erection of a temporary cover over the ruins of the Rotunda to protect them from weather damage, and he had taken measurements of the building, which would be necessary for reconstruction. The measurements were needed because the only drawings of the original building, held by Jefferson's great-granddaughter, Miss Ellen Randolph of Edgehill, showed few dimensions, though the drawings were made to scale on lined paper. These drawings had been made available to McDonald through the rector, Dr. W. C. N. Randolph, a great-grandson of Jefferson. The temporary cover and the measurements were properly done, according to the report of the building committee to the Board of Visitors on March 13, 1896. The fact that original drawings were loaned to McDonald, coupled with his charge by the board on November 4, shows that the board expected him to prepare drawings for reconstruction. The instructions accompanying his appointment could also have been expected to invite changes in the design. Though never credited, McDonald had developed features of the new Rotunda that were followed later by Stanford White.

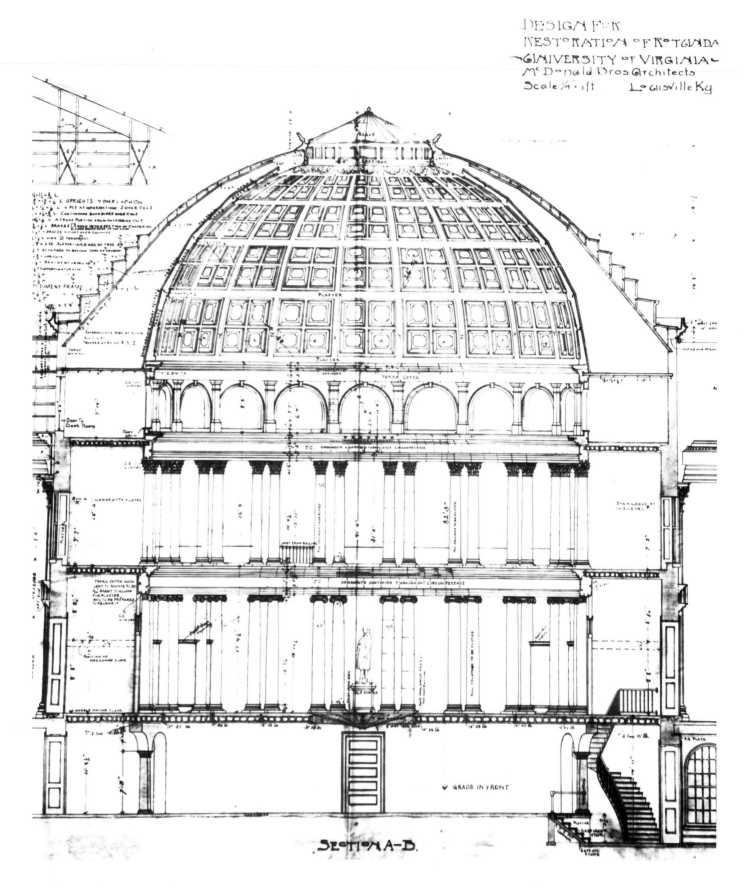

9. Rotunda section: drawing prepared by McDonald Brothers, Architects, for presentation to the building committee on January 4, 1896.

become apparent from McDonald's design that the Rotunda would require extensive changes to carry out the wishes of the university as expressed in the faculty report of October 31, 1895, and approved by the board on November 4. No further mention was made at this time of the faculty's efforts on November 20, 1895, to redirect the project. On January 15, 1896, the faculty met once again to press their opposition to any changes in the interior of the building. They adjourned and met again the next day to enact further resolutions to be presented to the board and to the building committee.

Stanford White's Design for the Rotunda

On January 18, 1896, at a meeting of the building committee, McDonald withdrew from the project, agreeing to reduce his fees by an amount equal to the cost of repairs to the flawed wings. Stanford White, of the firm of McKim, Mead & White, Architects, New York, was appointed architect for all the work to be done at the university.

White was not present at the meeting, but he visited the university on January 28 and 29, receiving at that time the specifications and the available drawings. He walked over the site and requested that a topographical drawing be made to assist in locating new buildings. The Rotunda drawings were still in the hands of McDonald Brothers in Louisville, who hastened to complete the partially finished preliminary plans, since the dimensions White needed were on these drawings. All drawings and the topographical study were forwarded to White by February 11. On February 21 he informed William Mynn Thornton (for the building committee) by telegram that the preliminary plans were ready for review by the committee. Only three weeks after his visit and no more than a week after receiving the dimensions for the Rotunda in the McDonald drawings, White had produced his ground plan showing three alternate locations for the new buildings and his rendering for the new Rotunda. The plans were sent to Thornton by express, and White attended a meeting of the building committee on March 2 to present them. With some revisions to reduce total costs, the Committee accepted the general plans as presented by White. (See fig. 10.) These were submitted to the Board of Visitors to consider during their meeting on March 13. When the board met on that day, a delegation of the faculty was present to express opposition to the White plan and to request once again that the interior of the Rotunda be returned to the form it had had before the fire. The board heard this recommendation but took no action. White then reported his plan, which was adopted by the board, and he was authorized to prepare detailed plans for release to prospective contractors for competitive bids. He began at once, and the drawings and specifications were ready for bidders by April 16. The contract was let on May 23 to Chas. H. Langley & Company of Richmond, Virginia.

When defending his proposed design on March 13 and in subsequent written statements, White contended that his exterior completed the Rotunda as Jefferson had wanted it, with a north portico that had been omitted strictly as an economy measure. That north portico had been added when the Annex was built. White argued that, inside the building, he was offering an ideal Rotunda that Jefferson would have preferred had funds been available to subdivide the interior for multiple purposes. These latter statements lacked support from any of Jefferson's documents, but they were highly

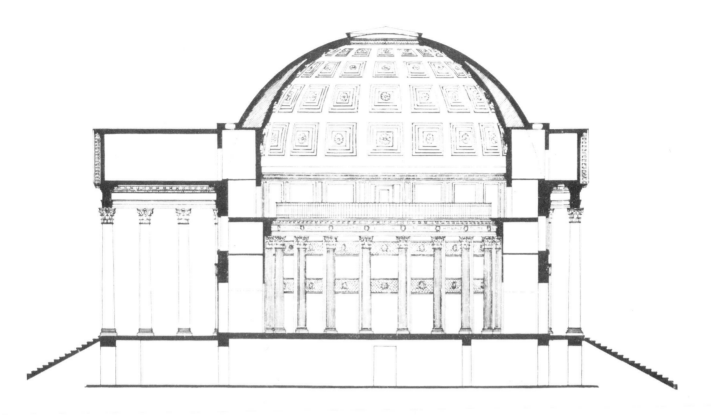

10. Rotunda section: drawing prepared by McKim, Mead & White, Architects, and presented to the building committee on March 2, 1896.

"To the question of remodeling of the interior of the Rotunda, we have given most careful study. Reasons of sentiment would point to the restoration of the interior exactly as it stood, but the dedication of the entire Rotunda to use as a Library, and the unquestionable fact that it was only practical necessity which forced Jefferson at the time it was built to cut the Rotunda in two stories, and that he would have planned the interior as a simple, single and noble room, had he then been able to do so, induces us to urge strongly upon your Board the adoption of a single dome room, as presented, not only as the most practical, but the proper treatment of the interior."

(Report of McKim, Mead & White to the Board of Visitors. See *Alumni Bulletin* O.S. 2 [1896]:139.)

persuasive coming from such a prominent architectural firm, which was renowned for its knowledge of neo-classical architecture.[14]

McKim, Mead & White had made previous studies of rotundas, and in 1893 McKim had designed the massive rotunda library at Columbia University in New York City.[15] In 1894, White had designed a somewhat smaller and more intimate rotunda for the new Bronx campus of New York University. This building became known as the Hall of Fame, and its design was echoed directly in White's design for the Rotunda at the University of Virginia. Both used columns of approximately three stories in height; both had Corinthian capitals and decoration of the entablatures. Both had coffered ceilings inside the domes, and White's initial rendering for the Virginia Rotunda very closely paralleled the New York University design. He had clearly adapted that plan to the dimensions of the Virginia building but had used brick columns covered by plaster—an economy measure at Virginia—for the marble columns he had used at New York University. White was offering his own design, not Jefferson's.

White argued on a number of occasions that he was

14. White's argument for his proposal was published in the *Alumni Bulletin*, (O.S. 2 [1896]:139). It was expanded in an article he wrote for *Corks and Curls* (the university yearbook), 11 (1898):127–30.

15. The three rotundas may be compared through their portrayal in *A Monograph of McKim, Mead and White, 1879–1915* (4 vols., New York: The Architectural Book Co., (n.d.) republished in 1973 as a single volume by Benjamin Blom, New York City). The design of Columbia University's library appears in plates 47–52, that of the NYU library in plates 75–77, and that of the University of Virginia in plates 110–112A. An introductory essay in the republished monograph invited comparison of the three buildings: "It would appear from the firm archives that White crystallized the NYU library design during 1894 or 1895 and began construction in June 1896, at the same time that he became involved in restoring the Jeffersonian rotunda itself in Charlottesville, Virginia" (p. 32).

11. Rebuilt Dome Room, ca. 1900.

"*The interior is a single room from the portico level up,
devoted entirely to the uses of the library. In addition to the
space on the main floor, there are three galleries, the topmost
at the springing of the dome being carried by a peristyle of
twenty columns. The room is finished in white, except the
ceiling, which is sky blue, picked out with stars. The decoration about the central light is a circle of eagles, modeled
from the figure in the ceiling of the hall at Monticello, the
eagles seeming to soar downward through the blue ether.*"

Alumni Bulletin, O.S. 5 [1898]:47.)

43

completing Jefferson's plans, and university officials seemed fully prepared to accept him as arbiter. Virtually all controversy ceased within the university (at least in statements to the public) as soon as White's design was accepted. Nearly five months of uncertainty over the future of the university, in terms of both structures that might be built and the financing necessary to complete them, was terminated by the decision. As John Thornton had suggested earlier, everyone could now cease their lamentations and look towards the future. At this point the university would enter the twentieth century with new and enlarged Grounds. There were so many features that had never been available before that details such as the changed interior of the Rotunda could be overshadowed by the general exhilaration and enthusiasm for the future.

When the newly reconstructed Rotunda opened in June of 1898, it housed a library in dry and fireproof quarters (fig. 11). Little argument was heard at this point about Jefferson's original design of the building having been lost. Photographs of the new exterior proudly displayed the north face with the new stairway and the esplanade that replaced the Annex. This was the Stanford White version of the Rotunda, giving it a new front facing the road from Charlottesville to Staunton. Previously the portion facing the Lawn, or south front, of the Rotunda had been considered its front—both in the Jefferson version and after Mills had added the Annex.

Whose Rotunda—
Jefferson's or White's?

*A*fter the Rotunda was reconstructed, writers in both the popular and the scholarly literature skirted the controversy over the new design in their attempts to achieve harmony within the university. Early writers knew the controversy, and some had been participants in it. They appeared to wish that the issues be laid to rest and, as a consequence, played down differences between Jefferson and White. To some extent, they interpreted the restoration of Jefferson's exterior of the building as the important point. Later writers appear to have blurred the distinctions even more, until finally, in the post–World War II period, readers could no longer distinguish differences between the two designs, from the literature then in print. A brief review shows some of the major stages in the development of that confusion.

In 1904, Paul B. Barringer—who had been chairman of the faculty from September 1896 until June 1903 and a strong advocate of returning the interior of the Rotunda to Jefferson's design—described the new construction as follows: "The group of buildings planned by Jefferson, and erected under his personal oversight, together with the recent additions made to harmonize with and complete his composition, constitutes what is undoubtedly the most characteristic and most artistic piece of academic architecture in America."[16]

Principals in the earlier controversy—including faculty advocates for the Jeffersonian design, Francis H. Smith, John W. Mallet, and Charles W. Kent—were still active members of the faculty in 1904. William Mynn Thornton and William H. Echols, faculty advocates of White's design, were still active. So was Armistead C. Gordon, who had been a member of the building committee during the postfire period, a supporter of the White design, and rector of the university during 1897–98—and who was still an active member of the Board of Visitors. Behind these leaders, other members of the university community had been aligned, and Barringer now concentrated on the positive aspects of university life.

A somewhat different approach was taken by John S. Patton in 1906. Patton praised the architects of the reconstruction of the university in general:

> *Ordinarily, restoration in matters of this kind is but another word for desecration, accomplished through the operation of bad taste or stinginess. Happily, the fire came when the reign of architectural horrors had ended. From that day to this good luck has seemed to attend the institution. Some wise person must have suggested McKim, Meade [sic] & White to the faculty, as the architects for this emergency,*

16. Paul B. Barringer, James M. Garnett, and Rosewell Page, eds., *University of Virginia: Its History, Influence, Equipment, and Characteristics* (New York: Lewis Publishing Co., 1904), 1:114.

and no doubt the same sage made fortunate suggestions to these gentlemen while they were studying the conditions and deciding upon the extent and manner of restoring what had been lost and of extending the original plant. The spirit of Jefferson dominated in this crisis, as it has at other crises, in the history of the University.

In this passage, Patton may be understood as praising the restoration of the Rotunda as well as the new buildings, and a few paragraphs later he specifically describes the exterior work on the Rotunda: "The Rotunda, already described to some extent, was rebuilt as far as its outward form was concerned in accordance with the original plans. This course was in obedience to the fitness of things and in response to a universal sentiment."[17]

Once again, Patton seems to have indicated general agreement concerning the restoration, but the most striking feature of his continuing discussion is that he does not once mention the interior treatment given the building by White. Furthermore, the previous description of the Rotunda, to which Patton refers in the quotation above, describes the Jeffersonian interior, drawing largely on a quotation from a paper by Francis H. Smith during the height of the controversy.[18] Patton's quotation is drawn from Smith's description of the interior of the building. Clearly, Patton was avoiding the controversy by merely keeping silent regarding the difficult points.

17. John S. Patton, *Jefferson, Cabell and the University of Virginia* (New York: The Neale Publishing Co., 1906), pp.288–89.
18. Ibid., p. 187. Francis H. Smith's article appeared in the *Alumni Bulletin*, O.S. 2(1895):85–90. Patton quotes the passage describing the interior of the building on pp. 88–89.

An account of the controversy was eventually published by Philip Alexander Bruce in his massive *History of the University of Virginia, 1819–1919*. Bruce was more open about the issues than were the earlier writers—as a full quarter century had passed since the fire. Some of the principals were dead; others were either inactive or in the twilight of their careers, and even they would not have been offended by Bruce's evenhanded descriptions. "The plan for the interior of the Rotunda was not in harmony with the original recommendation of the faculty, which had also received the approval of the Board—instead of that plan providing for the restoration of the two floors which had been laid down when the edifice was first built, it reduced the number to one. This one was to separate the great library room—which was to rise to the ceiling of the dome—from two large apartments in the basement, suitable for use as reference or reading rooms."[19]

This factual description was neutral enough, but Bruce concluded the passage with an assertion that was both unsupported and intended to settle any remaining questions about White's recommendations or the Board of Visitors' acceptance of them: "In counseling the adoption of this noble plan, the architect was, in reality, following the original wish of Jefferson, who had been only led to split up the area within the Rotunda by the imperative need of obtaining space for laboratories and lecture halls."[20]

Now the controversy was in the open, and presumably resolved. Barringer's silence and Patton's coy avoidance had been overcome. In the process, however, Bruce had claimed that there was no real issue, since

19. Bruce, *History* 4:276.
20. Ibid.

48

Jefferson and White were in agreement. The differences between the two architects were reduced to mere expediency and, therefore, to insignificance. With this claim, however, Bruce did lay to rest any serious questions about the design for almost forty years.

Later scholars did not go beyond the three main sources of secondary information described above. For example, in 1947, Karl Lehmann, gave no indication that Jefferson's interior of the Rotunda was different from the one that existed at the time of his writing. ". . . in the imitation of the Pantheon in Charlottesville, he did anything but schematically copy a model. Though in general he reduced the proportions of the building to one half of the original without modification, though he preserved the Corinthian order and other details of decoration, his changes are far reaching and very imaginative." Describing the interior, he continued:

> *Its interior, again, is loosely inspired by the prototype. With its unbroken colonnade and the extensively admitted light, it is a free invention made for the function of a library, and only the general dimensions of plan and elevation are preserved from the original. Naturally in the reduction to half size the bulky power of the Roman mass and the overwhelming grandeur of the interior of the Pantheon could not be duplicated. In the transformation resulting from the reduction and from the adaptation to the different function of a library, Jefferson has created a work of his own which will bear comparison with the Roman Pantheon, and in its animated and articulate vitality is something entirely different. In that sense it is more beautiful.*[21]

21. See Karl Lehmann, *Thomas Jefferson, American Humanist* (Chicago: University of Chicago Press, 1947), pp. 171–72.

This vague description drew heavily on Patton, who had gotten it from Francis H. Smith, but Lehmann does not mention Smith's article. Even more confusing, his description could be applied to either version of the building. Finally, he left the reader with no mention of White, but described Jefferson's design using verbs in the present tense. The effect of his description was a strong suggestion that one might then visit the university and see the Rotunda as Jefferson had intended it. Lehmann acknowledged the accounts of Bruce, Kimball, and Patton as sources on the Rotunda design, but he made no reference to the original drawings.

From this sampling of descriptions of the building by persons in several scholarly fields—and including those who are acknowledged for their studies of Jefferson and the University of Virginia—it is easy to see how the Rotunda designed by Stanford White might have been confused with Jefferson's original plans by those who were less familiar with the original drawings. Such was the case until Frederick Doveton Nichols began to stress the differences about 1955.

Uses of the Stanford White Rotunda

For forty years after the Rotunda reopened in 1898, it was the central library for the university. During that time the collection grew so that it filled this enlarged space and left it unduly crowded and inadequate for stack and study areas. When the university's present main library, the Alderman Library, was constructed and put into service in 1938, the entire collection housed in the Rotunda was removed to the new building. At the same time, relatively limited modifications and extensive maintenance were conducted to repair the ravages of time on the Rotunda. Terrace wings, external stairs, and the dome received extensive repairs. The work was done by the university's Department of Buildings and Grounds and was described in newspaper accounts in 1940 as the "second restoration."[22]

The Rotunda was no longer the central building of

22. *Baltimore Sun*, Sunday, January 14, 1940, sec. 2, p. 4. Professor Stanislaw Makielski, of the Department of Architecture, was named as being in charge of the work done by the Department of Buildings and Grounds.

12. Dome Room, about 1968, with library collection removed.

"The Rotunda exists solely as a symbol of its past glory and uses, and houses no function commensurate with its design or eminence of its concept."

(Report of Ballou and Justice, Architects, to the Rotunda Restoration Committee, May 8, 1969, quoted by Francis L. Berkeley, Jr., chairman, in a chronology of restoration prepared for the authors.)

the University, after its last major function—that of a library—had been removed (see fig. 12), although the building still contained a limited collection of artifacts of the old university and several minor administrative offices. The main room was the starting point for guided tours of the original grounds of the university and was also the site of occasional balls and receptions. The Rotunda stood, however, more as a monument to the past than as a central building (see fig. 13.) After World War II—when the university was engaged in a new round of expansion and the enrollment was increasing (as was the variety of offerings within the university)— further work on the Rotunda was overlooked in favor of new construction for other purposes.

The modern restoration efforts began in 1955, when President Colgate W. Darden, Jr., invited Professor Frederick D. Nichols to advise him on ways to enlarge Pavilion VIII—then the office of the president of the university—to house an expanded executive staff.[23] Nichols—who had been studying the Jefferson drawings of the university—was then engaged in efforts by the Garden Club of Virginia to restore the gardens behind the Lawns to Jefferson's original plans. He was also engaged in restoring the pavilions. He proposed as an alternative to expansion of Pavilion VIII that the Rotunda be returned to the Jefferson design, which

23. "In 1955, President Darden called me to his office to ask me to advise him on ways to expand Pavilion VIII, which had become too small for his staff. As an alternative, I suggested that he restore the Rotunda to Mr. Jefferson's design, which would give enough room for him and the Board of Visitors. Then Pavilion VIII could be returned to residential use." (Frederick D. Nichols, personal interview with the authors, May 11, 1978.)

13. The Rotunda, at this time, served mainly as a
picturesque backdrop for the Lawn, as in the special
Christmas lighting, 1972.

would yield the adequate space for offices that President Darden was then seeking. Nichols reports that President Darden was surprised to learn that the Rotunda, as he knew it, was not that of Jefferson. Darden's view, as reflected by Nichols, was a prevalent one within the university community, and it paralleled that expressed by Lehmann and other writers mentioned above.

Darden viewed a model prepared by Nichols's students, developed to show what the original Rotunda had been like, and he accepted the idea of restoring the building to its Jeffersonian design as a basis for planning. Nichols's argument, which Darden accepted, amounted to a reversal of the design process adopted by the faculty following the fire of 1895. Whereas the faculty had first designated the building as a library and had shaped its interior to suit, Nichols proposed that the Jeffersonian structure be restored and that suitable uses be found for the resulting building. He was confident that the building could once again become central to the life of the university. He and Darden agreed that this could be done by placing the offices of the president, his immediate staff, and the Board of Visitors in the building.

Planning
for Restoration

Darden proposed restoration of the Rotunda to the Board of Visitors, who endorsed it in 1957, provided it could be financed without use of funds normally available to the university. Nichols continued his research into the history of the building, including the Jefferson drawings and the related correspondence. William B. O'Neal conducted other studies in the Jefferson documents, publishing *Jefferson's Buildings at the University of Virginia: The Rotunda* in 1960. When Nichols and O'Neal began publishing the results of their studies of the Rotunda, suggestions were made publicly that the building should be restored to the Jeffersonian design. Many persons in the university community were reluctant to accept the claim that the Rotunda was not that originally designed by Jefferson. Others rejected the notion that any changes should be made in the existing building when the large sums necessary to finance the venture could be used so well in other ways.

By 1960 scarcely anyone alive remembered the Rotunda before the fire, and there were few who—even if they knew it had been changed by Stanford White—

understood why those changes were made or what the original design had been like. Still others were clearly concerned that money would be diverted from other important uses in the university toward a reconstruction that would have limited use and little interest to them personally or professionally.

Nichols relates that when he presented his suggestions to the Board of Visitors in 1955, a member of the board, a distinguished federal judge, commented that as a Visitor he had been accused of all sorts of desecrations in the university short of tearing down the Rotunda. He then asked Nichols whether that was what he was now being asked to support! The board approved the measure, however, and efforts were begun to raise funds for the restoration.

In the early 1960s, small sums of money were accumulated from special donations, and in 1964 the Jefferson Society and the Student Guide Service of the university, under the leadership of Mrs. Edwin M. Betts, initiated an annual Restoration Ball to raise funds. In 1965 the building was named a National Historic Landmark under the protection of the National Park Service, and it was listed in the National Register of Historical Buildings. In 1964 the General Assembly of Virginia appropriated $55,000 to replace the domed roof, which had been thought to be unsound.

Architect Louis W. Ballou,[24] of the firm Ballou and Justice, Architects, of Richmond, Virginia, was en-

---

24. Ballou had been a student at the university from 1923 to 1927, studying architecture under Professor Edmund S. Campbell. He had been interested in Jeffersonian architecture for many years and had directed the reconstruction of the State Capitol in Richmond. He considered the appointment as architect for restoration of the Rotunda a fitting climax to his career.

gaged to conduct an inspection of the roof for soundness and for its adherence to the Jeffersonian design. Ballou reported that the dome was structurally sound and that it followed the Jeffersonian design as closely as one might expect to achieve with contemporary methods.

President Edgar F. Shannon, Jr., who had succeeded Darden in 1959, appointed a committee of distinguished faculty members in 1965 to guide the planning. This committee, under the chairmanship of Francis L. Berkeley, Jr., turned their attention to the problem of search for legal and financial support for the reconstruction. On learning that the dome was sound and that it followed the Jeffersonian lines, the committee requested that the $55,000 be redirected to planning for restoration of the interior of the building. This proposal was accepted, and the General Assembly approved the altered use of the funds. On April 2, 1966, Ballou and Justice were retained to plan the restoration, and Nichols was retained as a consultant to the firm.

From the first, the committee was faced with decisions that required them constantly to balance the functional adaptation for future uses of the building against its historic essentials. Major renovation required that modern building, safety, and fire codes be observed. If the building were to be used as offices for the top-level administration of the university, it would have to include amenities to support that use. To be fireproof, the building would need significant changes in the structural supports throughout. In addition, there were now new materials that had been unavailable when the original building was being done, and some of the original materials would be expensive and difficult to obtain. The same thing would be true of workmen's skills. (Eventually, skilled workmen had to be brought from New York and Baltimore as well as coming from Virginia.)

Plans for the new restoration were completed in 1971 and were approved by both the Board of Visitors and the Virginia Commission for the Arts. In the meantime there was a continuing search for funds to carry out the work. Nichols felt that one major source was the Cary D. Langhorne Trust of Washington, D.C., which included a substantial sum designated for the restoration of Jeffersonian buildings at the university. These funds, however, would need to be matched by very substantial amounts from other sources before work could be undertaken.

An unexpected source of matching funds developed in the United States Department of Housing and Urban Development in 1972. Access to HUD funds came most unexpectedly, when Nichols, attending a luncheon in Washington, D.C., found himself seated next to a HUD official. The event is described in the *Washington Star-News* on April 1, 1974, as follows:

> *The man from HUD happened to mention his agency's new little-known fund for historic preservation. Nichols happened to mention the Rotunda project.*
> *A few months later it was all worked out. The Langhorne Trust and HUD each are paying $1.1 million for the restoration work.*

These funds were formally granted to the university in a ceremony at Monticello on April 28, 1972. Articles in the *Charlottesville Daily Progress* on April 29 and in another Charlottesville paper, the *Jefferson Journal*, on May 4 described the ceremonies, which were attended by Patricia Nixon, representing her father, the president of the United States. Presentation was made by Floyd H. Hyde, assistant secretary for community development for HUD, and by Carroll A. Mason, HUD area director, of Richmond, Virginia. Hyde commented that he knew Mr. Jefferson must be very pleased. His statement was quoted in the *Jefferson Journal*, as follows: "The presence of all of us here today is a small token of the respect and admiration we have for this great University and its founder. It is also an example of how government and its people can work together to preserve the great heritage that pervades our history."

With $2,200,000 from the grants by HUD and the Langhorne Trust plus $55,000 previously appropriated by the General Assembly and approximately $16,000 from other gifts, the work of restoration could begin. Plans were then hurried through to have the work begun in time for the building to be dedicated during the first bicentennial year of 1976.

Technical Questions in Restoration

Any work of restoration—whether it be an authentic and precise reproduction of the original work in detail, or a restoration of the originator's concept, with some freedom to modify detail—is a product of complex judgments. Twice before the present effort, the Rotunda had been "restored." Stanford White's work had been called a restoration, even though he had deviated markedly from the details of Jefferson's original interior. He had argued vigorously, however, that his was a restoration of Jefferson's building in style and structure, but with materials then available to meet specific functional purposes. The relatively minor work done in 1939–40 to repair the roof and wings, was also called a restoration, even though the project never approached in extent either the White effort or the work undertaken between 1973 and 1976.

This 1970s restoration once again raised questions concerning the authenticity of the return to the Jeffersonian design. The new set of functions, plus new requirements for construction, would require adaptation of the building, and from the beginning the project

63

was known formally as the Restoration and Adaptation of the Rotunda.

It seems appropriate to an understanding of the task to review briefly the questions and issues raised during the preparation of plans, and to identify those that could be addressed only when construction was underway. We have already mentioned the question about the safety of the Dome, which had been raised in the initial stages of consideration and was adequately resolved by the inspection of the double dome.

Ballou and his engineers had tapped holes in the inner dome and had walked around in the annular spaces between the inner and outer domes, examined the metal straps that provided tensile force to keep the building walls from spreading; and compared the elevation of the dome with the original Jefferson drawings. This set of studies was essential before any structural work could be planned, and the answering of questions related to the dome could then proceed early enough to define the limits of the task. The exterior of the dome would receive some minor changes, as the step rings were to be modified to return the exterior lines from the five variable steps provided by Stanford White to seven, the number in the original design—thus restoring more of a spherical visual effect, whereas White's version had left the roof with more of a conical appearance.

Other questions remained to be answered about the dome. A new waterproof skylight would be installed, following the dimensions of Jefferson's skylight, and the exterior weather surface would be renewed, replacing the deteriorating copper. Though both the original building and White's modifications were profusely documented, there were loose ends and missing bits of information. For example, there were no drawings showing how the dome had actually been built by White. All of his drawings showed an earlier version of the dome, one that was not actually built, and there were none to show the changes made after the original plan was approved by the board. One drawing in the university's archives contained notes, dated 1940, from the university's Department of Buildings and Grounds that said, "Actual construction," but reliable information could be gained only by measurements. Even the size of the skylight was not recorded accurately on White's drawings. Dimensions were given, but these were contradictory and on obsolete versions of the drawings. Only field measurements would suffice for the new work.

Carrying forward the sleuthing necessary in the early studies, Ballou examined a bill of materials issued by Jefferson's proctor, Arthur Spicer Brockenbrough, for replacement panels of glass with trapezoidal shapes that could fit only into the skylight. By carefully examining their dimensions, he was able to calculate the number of panes in the original skylight and the conical form of the light. Then these dimensions were used to design the new skylight. Because there had always been a problem with breakage and with sealing, the new skylight was fabricated of steel with plexiglass, painstakingly sealed to prevent leakage.

Another bit of necessary detective work was related to the color of the exterior dome. No specifications could be found to show what color the dome had been painted originally, but bills of material showed that all paint purchased for the original Rotunda was white. Since the entire dome had been consumed in the fire, there were no samples that could be examined. Reference to early photographs and sketches of the building showed that at different times the dome had been painted in dark colors. In addition, some persons liked the soft copper patina that had covered the Stanford White dome and wanted it continued in the restoration. Eventually, a test was made by painting sections of the dome in these colors, and at one stage of reconstruction, the roof took on a harlequin appearance.

Other questions were raised during reconstruction. One of these related to flooring. The building committee had decided that the new floors at portico and Dome Room levels should duplicate, as far as possible, the heart pine of the original, and they sought a source of such wood. Raymond C. Power, a friend of Ballou's, had a hobby of collecting wood from old buildings that had been demolished. He made his collection available for use in this project, so the materials were as close to those of the original as could be obtained. There was also a question about the direction in which the boards should be laid. Should they run from fireplace to fireplace and be seen crossing one's view as one entered the Dome Room from the stairway? Or should they be laid away from the stairway to the opposite side of the room?

After much debate about the merits of each direction, an old photograph of the Dome Room settled the question by showing the direction as being from fireplace to fireplace (fig. 14).[25]

25. The photograph was lent to the committee by Mr. Jerry Showalter, manager of Newcomb Hall Bookstore at the University of Virginia. He did not know that the search was underway to find this particular detail, but he had purchased a photographic album at an auction of the effects of Kenneth Brown because the album contained interesting old photographs, including a number taken at the university in the winter of 1890. This snapshot of the Jefferson statue showed clearly that the boards in the floor of the Dome Room ran from fireplace to fireplace.

Discoveries of this type occurred repeatedly as interested persons, knowing that the committee was using old photographs as sources of detailed information, made their collections available.

14. Snapshot of the Dome Room in 1890, by Kenneth
Brown. This photograph gave the only positive evidence that floorboards had originally run from fireplace
to fireplace.

This was the only conclusive information found to settle the question, as there were no original drawings or notes showing how it had been done. The search had been initiated long before construction began, but the answer was found only after the construction was underway, although before the time had come to actually lay the floors.

A similar question faced the builders about the pattern of bricks in the basement floor. Should they be laid in conventional squares, in a herringbone pattern, or in some other arrangement? Extensive research was inconclusive on this point, and after the usual debates, a decision had been made to lay them in a square pattern. On the morning when the actual work was ready to begin, a workman—clearing out an edge as a starting point—discovered a small section of old brick floor laid in a herringbone pattern. A hurried conference of the building committee, the architects, and the contractor concluded that the original plan should be followed, and within minutes, the work was underway, using the herringbone pattern.

Another question had to do with interior cornices in the various rooms. Records showing the locations of cornices could be found only for the museum that had been the chemistry laboratory. References by Jefferson to Palladio's drawings showed some of the cornices chosen for the building, but no mention was made of the rooms for which each had been selected. Nichols conducted research on cornices but found no clear record in Jefferson's letters concerning the question of which cornices went in which rooms in the Rotunda. From these studies, however, he determined the possible choices for each room. This small sampling gives some idea of the types of technical questions that had to be addressed during the restoration.

Another set of questions faced the restorers as they dealt with adaptive use. Some of these adaptations would be related to the amenities needed for persons using the building; still others would be required by building codes that were nonexistent in Jefferson's day. A brief listing of some of those questions will indicate the nature of the problems. First, climate control was to be provided by air conditioning, with controlled temperature and humidity. This equipment had to be installed unobtrusively, and adequate distribution ducts had to be placed in the building. A second problem was that of echoes and reverberations of sound, which had always plagued users of the Dome Room. Complaints had been common in both the Jefferson Dome Room and the White Dome Room about the terrible acoustics that tormented those who performed or lectured there. The restorers had to solve this problem by improving on the original acoustical properties.

Another modern concern was the delivery of materials to the several floor levels and access to different floors by handicapped persons. An elevator was specified for the new building, to be placed in one of the openings formerly used as a small staircase. A part of the restoration would return the Jeffersonian broad stairways eliminated in the Stanford White design; these would require careful study of dimensions of the building in order to secure balustrade designs as nearly like the original as possible, but at the same time the stairways needed to be adequately fireproof for safe access to the upper levels.

There were questions as to how the building was lighted originally, since surviving documentation showed only the skylights provided by Jefferson and his recommendation that Argand lights be used.[26]

For the restored building, Argand-styled chandeliers were selected from a design that Jefferson had liked and that had been used in the old House of Representatives Building in Washington, D.C. Indirect lights with rheostat controls were selected to provide light in the alcoves and balconies.

Fire and safety regulations required that a rail be installed around the intermediate balcony if persons were to be permitted to enter that level. This was an alteration from the Jefferson design.

Another safety feature required was the installation of exit signs and of panic bolts on the doors. Ingenious efforts made these features serve their intended purposes of safety and yet not obtrude unduly in the restored building. Electrical controls and various items needed for operation of the building were placed in the closets in the free-form hallways and were made to disappear as nearly as possible into the walls. Automatic sprinklers were inconspicuously inserted in walls and the dome. Curved doors were used, following the lines of the wall and trimmed so as to be nearly invisible. Special latches were installed so that the doors could be opened or closed by merely pushing against them.

Finally, there were decisions related to the furnishings—the carpets, the furniture, and the like—which

26. Argand lights, named for their inventor, Aimé Argand, a Swiss physicist and mathematician, burned whale oil. They were designed so that a current of air, rising in the center of the flame, steadied the flame and thus produced much more light than candles or other sources then available.

were largely chosen for the uses for which the restored building had been intended. Most all of these features that we have cited in relation to adaptation either were merged with the structure as unobtrusively as possible or were provided in ways that could allow future removal without disturbing the lines of the Jeffersonian structure.

Controversies Aroused by Restoration

We have already mentioned the technical questions that required research for the restoration of this building. Additional decisions were required to balance restoration and adaptation. We have also reviewed the confusion between the Stanford White and the Jefferson designs, which led to some people's feeling that the work should not be undertaken, and we have commented on questions surrounding financial commitment to this task.

From the time Nichols published an article in 1961 proposing restoration of the building until a few weeks before it was dedicated, the Rotunda was the subject of policy discussions. The purists pointed out that the Rotunda could never be exactly restored and that it was a waste of time and money to attempt such a thing: Put the building in good shape, and leave it alone; to do more would deceive the public and compound past mistakes.

Others, who were sensitive to public and private needs of the underprivileged, urged that the money be devoted to charitable purposes. The university, how-

73

ever, was using money previously designated exclusively, by both the Cary D. Langhorne Trust and the U.S. Department of Housing and Urban Development for historic restorations.

Debates were long and often heated, extending until late 1976—even after the building was opened. In the early days the controversy centered around the principle of restoration. In a letter to the *Cavalier Daily*, November 3, 1965, J. J. Thomas, historian of the Student Guides Service, supported the restoration, claiming that Stanford White's rebuilding of the Rotunda was the cause of its standing unused and of its being architecturally unacceptable. In support of his argument, Thomas recited the changes made by White and discussed the aesthetics of his design. "White's grandiose 'railroad station classic' is a poor substitute for the exquisite Corinthian detail used by Mr. Jefferson. Since the library outgrew the Rotunda in the 1930's it has been used as a temporary office building. It is a shame that the finest building designed by Mr. Jefferson should be allowed to remain in this state."

In the same issue of the *Cavalier Daily*, Dr. John D. Forbes, former editor of the *Journal of the Society of Architectural Historians* and professor of business history in the Graduate School of Business Administration at the University of Virginia wrote:

> *It is time to take a calm and thoughtful look at the proposal now current to restore the interior great hall of the Rotunda as a facsimile of the original Jeffersonian fabric.*
>
> *This proposal has been offered primarily in terms of authenticity and tradition, both strong and often valid factors. Neglected from the discussion, however, in addition to alternative uses for the considerable sum of money involved, has been the consideration of aesthetics. I submit that the present magnificent Rotunda chamber with its full sweep,*

74

> *from main level to oculus, a view gained after ascending the*
> *monumental exterior staircases, is a far grander concept*
> *than the original construction of a low ceilinged main floor,*
> *cut up into oval offices, plus a second, truncated dome room*
> *reached by furtive little staircases at the edges.*

Spirited exchanges continued. Mrs. Charles M. Davison, Jr. (Alida Wilson, class of 1934, and daughter of the late Dean James Southall Wilson), in a letter published in *Richmond Times-Dispatch* of March 16, 1966, added:

> *The Rotunda was a beautiful library as Mr. White*
> *designed it. It could become the most beautiful undergraduate*
> *library in the country. Fix the plaster and the sagging roof,*
> *update the seating and bookshelves, install the elevator service*
> *and steps to beautiful tiers of books on the balconies all the*
> *way to the dome. Make it again what Mr. Jefferson planned*
> *and Mr. White designed, the library center of undergraduate*
> *life at the University of Virginia.*

Meanwhile, the university committee consulted outside experts who rejected the Rotunda as being too small for use as an undergraduate library.

On September 22, 1973, architectural critic Wolf Eckardt published a facetious letter in the *Washington Post* in the name of Thomas Jefferson, addressed to President-elect Frank L. Hereford, Jr.,

> *Let us not, dear sir, speak of faithful restoration of*
> *"Jefferson's Rotunda"; the well-intentioned adaptations are far*
> *more likely to result in mutilations of my design. . . .*
> *Let the Rotunda, then, not be "restored" but repaired.*
> *Let it serve not administrative governing but as a center*
> *of academic pursuits and recreation of our students. They are*
> *the central purpose of the very life of the University. Earth,*
> *as I have said, is for the living. . . .*

The most regular organized opposition to the project was through the student newspaper and the Student Council. Council fought for use of the building by students, arguing that if they were excluded, there was no way the building could be considered as central to the life of the university. Their voices eventually converged on the question of use, so that the intended plan of using the building to house the president's office was abandoned when Shannon retired to return to teaching and Hereford was installed as president. The debate continued, however, as the Student Council sought clarification on alternate proposed uses. The council also distrusted the statements that the administration had renounced use of the building to house the president's offices.

On April 10, 1974, after Hereford's announcement, the *Cavalier Daily* published an article showing a sketch of the free-form hall on the main floor, divided by a steel and glass partition at the base of the stairs, for fire protection. Author Dusty Melton asked why such a screen was needed if no offices for the president were to be there. Did the continuing presence of this screen suggest that other, perhaps lesser, administrative offices would be placed there? He noted the installation of a private bath in the west oval room as further evidence that the building might yet be used as office space.

On April 19, the *Cavalier Daily* quoted Shannon as saying that "there has been 'an absolute and legal commitment' to house the President's office in the Rotunda since the restoration program was promised $2.1 million in federal and private grants two years ago." An editorial in the same issue, entitled "The President's Rotunda" quoted Shannon as saying that when the restoration was completed in 1976, his successor as president would have been in office for two years, and by that time there would be new members of the Board of Visitors and new student leaders. These people could make their own assessments and their own choices.

When Hereford succeeded Shannon as president, he appointed the Historic Central Grounds Committee to consider the question of uses for the Rotunda. This committee of faculty and the Student Council Committee on Uses for the Rotunda continued to discuss issues related to uses until the spring of 1976, only weeks before the work of the contractor was completed.

On December 5, 1975, the *Cavalier Daily* writers were still worrying over the possible uses of the building for offices:

> *The main floor oval rooms simply are not suited for administrative office space. They are entities unto themselves, unsuitable for secretaries and typewriters and Xerox machines and ringing telephones all competing in a single void. After the finally retracted proclamations last year that the Rotunda would house the office of the University President and that a glass fire screen wouldn't divide the "dumb-bell" room on the main level such a decision to house administrative offices—for whatever length of time—is simply unacceptable.*

Not until March 1976 did the newspaper announce that the differences between the Historic Central Grounds Committee and Executive Vice-President Avery Catlin's office (speaking for the administration) had been resolved over use of the building—then scheduled to be turned over to the university the following month. Even after the building opened, questions about use of the building continued to be raised, and conditions and fees for scheduled uses were points of contention.

Catlin was quoted in the *Cavalier Daily*, March 16, 1976, as saying that the final plan followed closely a report developed by the Student Council committee, though the wording had been changed. Council's committee had listed a set of activities deemed suitable for the building, including meetings of the Board of Visitors, the Student Council, the Honor Committee, and the Faculty Senate; occasional meetings of small classes; and special events such as important presidential activities, University Guide Service historical displays, lectures, art displays, concerts, banquets and other distinguished social events. Of the regularly scheduled events anticipated in this list, only the Board of Visitors meetings were ultimately to be held in the building. Most of the occasional events mentioned were permitted, however, and a scheduling service was provided.

At issue was the protection and care of the building and its expensive and elegant furnishings, exposed to use by many members of the university community. With the location there of the president's office removed from consideration and with the prospect of occasional use of the building by reservation, problems of supervision and maintenance had been intensified.

II

The Work of Restoration and Adaptation

The Work of Restoration and Adaptation

*H*aving briefly reviewed the history of the Rotunda, we shall now share visually, with the reader, the delights of the building upon its completion in 1976. We shall go behind the scenes to show in color the major stages of the restoration and adaptation.

The modern conveniences added to the building provide for the comfort and safety of the building without too much intrusion on the aesthetics. At the same time, the free-form staircase, the glistening wooden floors, and the molding and cornices in the style of the eighteenth century suggest the atmosphere in which our forebears lived and worked.

The first section discusses the preparation for the restoration of the building; the second, the construction; and the last, the dedication.

15. Preparation of the interior required demolition of
the Stanford White alterations, January 1974.

Preparation

*F*red Warner, construction superintendent for R. E. Lee & Son, Inc., sounded the keynote for this section when he observed: "[Stanford] White changed the whole thing around and now it's our job to put it back."[1]

Mention has previously been made of the careful research, sleuthing, and planning that took place throughout the project. Concerns about the safety of the dome and many other details about column capitals, skylight shape, herringbone brick, and cornice selection were resolved only after the most careful observation and discussion.

During the preparation phase, the contractor worked carefully to remove the Stanford White interior without damaging parts of the original building that had withstood the fire. He also preserved the entire exterior—dome, walls, porticoes, windows, and doorways. As a result, all plaster, mortar, bricks, and steel from the Stanford White interior were removed piece

1. "Rotunda Supervisor Improves on Jefferson," *Charlottesville Daily Progress*, May 25, 1975, p. C–1.

83

16. Down came column capitals and the galleries,
November 1973.

by piece, and the rubble was collected for removal through windows and doors, usually in wheelbarrows (fig. 15). As work progressed through the winter of 1973–74 and the early spring, the grand neoclassical interior of the building was transformed into a cavernous, dark, and coliseum-like circular structure. At times, dust from the demolition so filled the air that one could scarcely see details of the far interior of the building; yet the work continued. (See figs. 16 and 17.) Down came steel balconies, plaster, and brick columns and eventually Stanford White's tile floor of the Dome Room. All plaster was removed from the walls so that the structure was revealed in its starkest and barest condition. Many features of the building long covered within the walls were exposed, including gas and electric lines that had been added, probably in 1896, in recesses in the exterior walls to carry lighting and utilities to the upper levels. (See figs. 18–20.)

There were surprising discoveries, such as the pair of small fireplaces, or ovens, recessed in the north wall of the east oval room in the basement (fig. 21), apparently installed during original construction to equip the room for chemistry lectures and demonstrations. These small fireplaces—placed side by side and each about fifteen inches wide and less than two feet high—still held shards of melted glass and bits of burned wood and charcoal from the 1895 fire. There was no record of their presence, and they had been completely covered over in the Stanford White reconstruction. The fireplaces may be seen today in the museum room through a pair of small doors that cover their openings. Professor Raymond C. Bice, Jr., chairman of the Rotunda Restoration Committee after July 1, 1974, commented on the discoveries made by workmen during the course of the project, "I was just amazed at the intelligence of the

workmen. They would call things to our attention, because sometimes the evidence was in nooks and crannies where neither the contractor nor any of us had been. They were crawling back in there, and they would come out and report" (personal interview, April 18, 1978).

Another fascinating discovery occurred when White's four small circular stairways to the balconies were removed, exposing the original brick installed under Jefferson's direction. It had been assumed that stairways had always been located in the spaces where the flat facades of the south and north porticoes stand out from the circular building. Inspection showed, however, that all but one of the openings had been left unfinished and irregular in shape until White used them for the small staircases.

The large spaces in the corners produced by the facades were probably left open by Jefferson's builders because little structural advantage would have been gained by filling them and a considerable amount of material would have been required to do so. Original drawings showed no staircases in these locations, and one of the spaces is marked to show its intended use as a shaft for clock weights.

According to Ballou, only the opening in the southwest corner showed evidence of having contained a stair before White's remodeling, and that only from the basement to the main floor. When this area was exposed during demolition of the White portion of the building, remnants of charred wood showed a door frame and the ends of stair treads damaged by fire and covered during the reconstruction. These pieces remain visible at the basement level just west of the entrance door.

87

17. Dust from demolition filled the air, January 1974.

"*The entire interior of the Rotunda had to be removed without disturbing the exterior, and all materials needed . . . had to be moved in or out . . . through existing doors and windows.*"

(R. E. Lee & Son, Inc., report to Associated General Contractors of America [AGC], January 1977, p. 3.)

"*This work naturally had to be done with a great deal of care, since all that was left after the demolition was accomplished was a silo about 80 feet tall and 75 feet in diameter; the exterior which was constructed of brick that had been through a fire of 1895, was none too safe after the two floors had been removed.*"

(Louis W. Ballou to Associated General Contractors of America, January 6, 1977; copy in R. E. Lee & Son, Inc., report to AGC.)

89

18, and 19. Architect Ballou inspects demolition, December 1973. Red paint on the walls marks the location of future installations.

20. Bare walls revealed long-hidden steel supports, stairway openings, and utility passages (dark line on the left), January 1974.

21. Ovens used in the chemistry laboratories before the fire of 1895 were exposed during demolition, September 1974.

22. Dome repairs were superficial, April 1974.

Throughout the early phases of the demolition, much attention was paid to the dome (fig. 22). Ballou noted: "We certainly satisfied ourselves, and I think we satisfied everybody who had seen the drawings . . . that Mr. White's dome and Mr. Jefferson's dome were within a few inches of each other, and if we had to take off Mr. White's dome and replace it with another, we couldn't put it back any closer than Mr. White had" (personal interview, February 16, 1978).

The skylight was removed (fig. 23), as was the copper roof, revealing the tiled dome, so the seven stepped rings could be restored to the dome shape designed by Jefferson (fig. 24).

Masses of rubble gave convincing proof that the demolition had been orderly and complete (fig. 25). Practically all of the job had to be done by hand and small machinery, and this is one of the marvels of the project.

Stanford White's Rotunda was gone. Removal of the eagles and stars from the ceiling (fig. 26) symbolized the return of Jefferson's simple design for the interior of the dome. The first phase of the task had been completed (fig. 27).

23. The leaking skylight was removed, October 1974.
White had installed an enlarged skylight over the large
Dome Room, so removal of the old skylight allowed
a return to the original dimensions in the new one.

24. New steps were installed on the dome, returning to the proportions Jefferson had used. In this photograph (October 1974), one can also see that student pranksters had left their marks on the roof, with spray-painted names of their dormitories: "Bonnycastle tops Hancock."

25. Debris from the old skylight, October 1974.

26. Interior scaffolds reached up to the ceiling and the skylight, October 1974.

27. The coliseum-like interior rose all the way up from
the main floor, July 1974.

Construction

There was a brief lull in the activity as the Rotunda was silent and bare; then the hustle and bustle of construction became evident everywhere. The west arcade was temporarily opened (fig. 28), and supplies arrived in an orderly stream. (See fig. 29.) The restoration of Jefferson's Rotunda had begun.

Step by step the oval rooms and the Dome Room would once more appear as indicated in the Nichols models. Francis L. Berkeley, Jr., writing in the *Alumni News*, July-August 1972, voiced everyone's hopes: "The future visitor to the Rotunda will see at the center of the University, in place of the empty shell, a building functioning significantly in accordance with the genius of its original design."

While the restoration of any building is an exacting process, the Rotunda was exceptional because of its unique history and symbolic interest. As they were exposed, old parts had to be studied, to determine whether they could stay or would require replacement. Measurements had to be taken to fit new parts to old, and, above all, the blending of old and new had to

28. The west arcade was opened temporarily to give
access for removal of debris and delivery of materials,
December 1973.

29. From the top of the dome, gardens and construction areas gave contrasting views, October 1974.

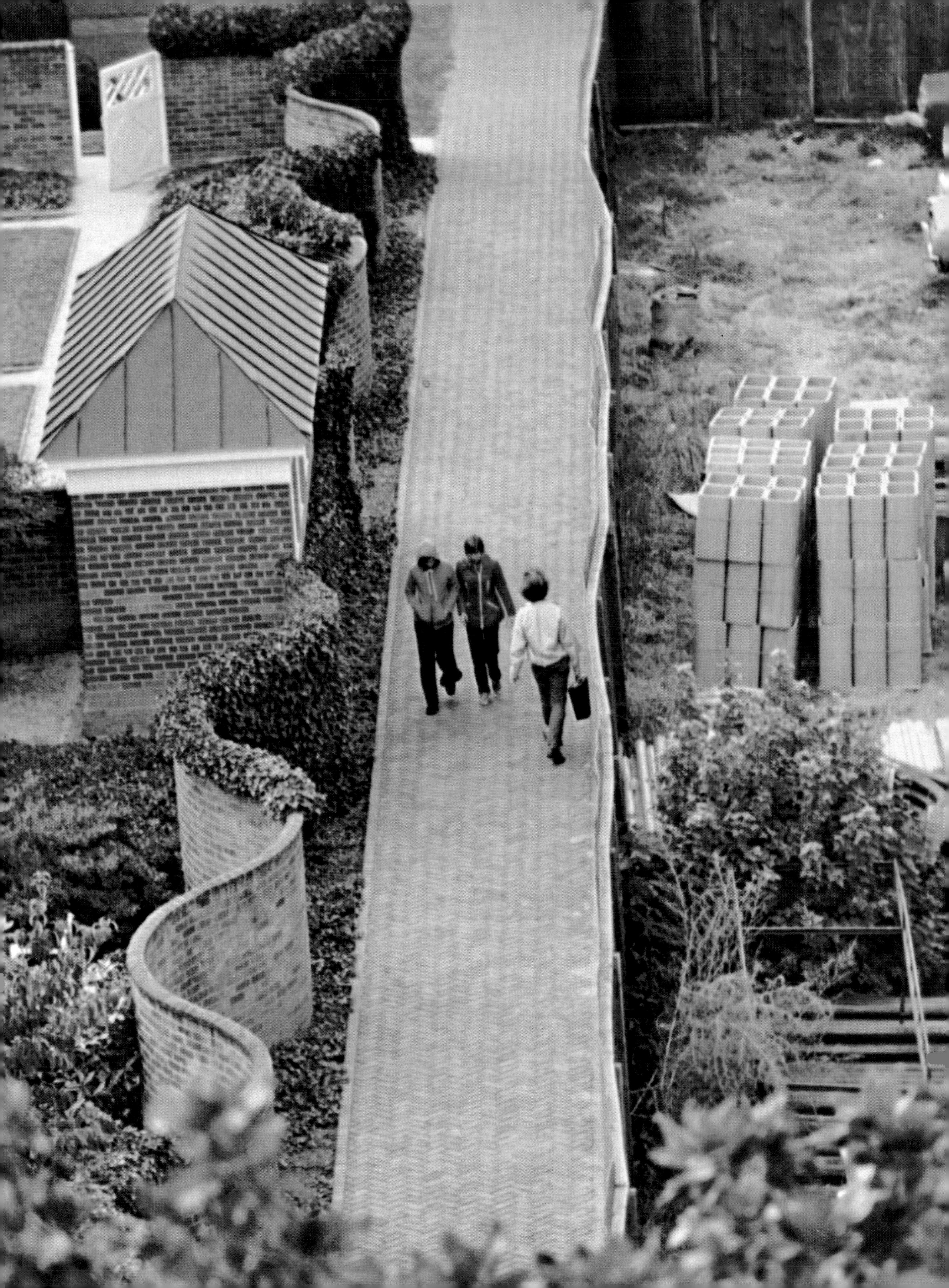

30. The first two columns for the Dome Room arrive,
April 1975.

31. Plasterer prepares curved cornice in the Dome
Room, April 1975.

create a new unity that justified the effort. The restoration was also adequately funded, an advantage not enjoyed by White, so all parties felt a special obligation to get it right.

Able and sensitive workmen were involved, and each seemed to feel personal responsibility for the task; contractor, architect, and restoration committee were in constant attendance. Bice recalls that the committee was consulted on decisions about details, "sometimes two or three times a day." It was frequently difficult to tell in advance which decisions were minor, with simple consequences, and which had major implications. Some could be planned well in advance, but others required quick response to avoid interruption of the work schedule.

Construction requires intricate orchestration of materials and workmen, each ready for a special role at just the right time and place. Seldom is the task of coordination as evident as it was in the Rotunda, however, where space limitations and protection from the weather required that materials be stored very close to the working area. For example, in figure 30, which shows the arrival of the first two columns, we see that what appears at first glance to be a cluttered and chaotic Dome Room floor was actually highly organized. Crates of column capitals and pedestals were carefully arranged around the periphery of the room, even as plasterers overhead were running the Tuscan cornices (fig. 31). The two columns, just delivered, lay in a central position on the floor, awaiting inspection and measurement. If we had looked out of the windows, we would have noted it was a rainy April afternoon, and all these materials were well protected. Such matters are always on a contractor's mind.

32. From the dome, where new roof is being installed, workmen had a clear view over Brooks Museum and Charlottesville, December 1974.

33. The new skylight was in place; furring strips covered the dome in preparation for the new metal roof, December 1974.

Each part of the construction now had to be fitted into the whole. (See figs. 32 and 33.) In a personal interview on February 16, 1978, Ballou told us how he had been able to determine the original form of the skylight:

> *"We had no information on the shape of the [original] skylight—how many divisions it had or anything about the slope. We did know that its diameter was shown as sixteen feet on Mr. Jefferson's drawing of the Dome Room. We also knew that Mr. Jefferson had built a skylight that didn't last very long and leaked almost immediately. . . . We found . . . that Mr. Brockenbrough [the university's proctor during the original construction] had ordered three trapezoidal shaped pieces of glass to replace three pieces broken in the skylight. The largest dimension of one of these pieces was over two feet, so we assumed that was the largest piece used. From that assumption we could calculate the number of panels and the height of the skylight. [See fig. 34.]*

The Old Clock was retained, and through its face can be seen the Lawn and Cabell Hall (fig. 35). A clock was specified for the south portico by Jefferson, and following the fire, a new one was given by Jefferson M. Levy. Dr. Paul B. Barringer, chairman of the faculty from 1896–1903, gives a delightful account of the clock in his memoir, *The Natural Bent* (Chapel Hill: The University of North Carolina Press, 1949, p. 207.)

> *Soon after recovering from the fever I, with several other students, volunteered to help the Monticello Guard out of a difficulty. They were to be inspected and were unable to muster a sufficient number of members to pass, so—as I had been drilled as a cadet at Bingham's [Prep School] and happened to fit a spare uniform—I was selected among others. The inspector was well pleased, and we were allowed to carry our "Spencer rifles" up to the University, subject to*

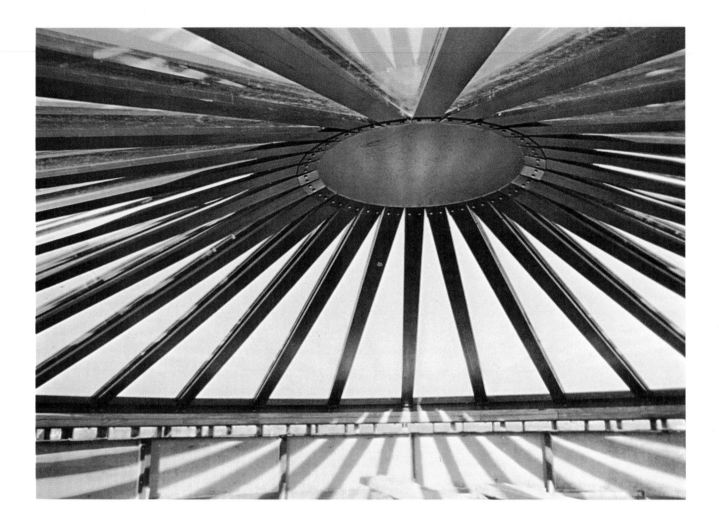

34. Interior of the new skylight, December 1974.

call. Securing a little ammunition, we took potshots from an upper room in House E [Dawson's Row], thus breaking the usual academic calm. Our favorite target was the clockface on the Rotunda, which was well peppered before the guns were recalled. By standing far back in the room, no telltale smoke came forth, and we risked only one or two shots a day, but soon "Old Harry" [Professor James F. Harrison] the Chairman [of the faculty, 1873–86] was tearing his hair. Twenty-odd years later when the University was presented with a new clock, I, as chairman, ordered a bullet-proof face, a unique order at that time.

Utilities for the Rotunda were placed inconspicuously in the attic of the south portico, beneath the steps of the north portico, in the basement, and in a new access tunnel beneath the floor of the basement. The trench for the tunnel was dug twelve feet beneath the floor in hitherto undisturbed red clay, along the north-south diameter of the building. Figure 36 shows workmen placing forms for the poured walls in May 1974.

Local plasterers ran continuous curved cornices, and they prepared supports for premolded decorations to be applied later. Throughout the building, plasterers had to follow curved walls and cornices, and frequently the constantly changing curves in the oval and hour-glass shaped rooms.

Column shafts and bases were manufactured from wood by Knipp and Company of Baltimore and were shipped to the job site for fitting and assembling. The wooden shaft of one of each pair of columns was split to allow installation around a steel load-bearing post (figs. 37 and 38).

35. The Lawn and Cabell Hall through the face of the clock, December 1974.

36. The new utilities tunnel, twelve feet below the basement floor, May 1974.

37. Columns were shipped in sections and assembled in place, September 1975.

38. Prefabricated column base, awaiting installation, July 1975.

39. Installation of columns, September 1975.

40. Handrail for intermediate balcony being welded into place, July 1975.

The workers set the base and shaft using a wooden frame to hold the capital. This was cast in plaster, as an inexpensive copy of capitals carved from black locust in Jefferson's original Dome Room (fig. 39).

The intermediate balcony had had no handrail in its original form, but safety regulations required the installation of one in the restoration (fig. 40). At least one drawing of the original Rotunda shows the old balcony without any handrails, but with books arranged along the edge of the balcony. Later photographs of balconies show cases placed against the walls but still no handrails.

There were numerous tasks that were essential, but not self-evident in the completed building. For example, visitors to the Rotunda admire the balustrade that forms part of the entablature over the columns in the Dome Room. They seldom guess that during construction, workmen installed the prefabricated sections like some enormous toy. (See fig. 41.)

Stair-trim detail was forecast by a small sample tacked to the curved stairway leading up to the Dome Room (fig. 42). Such samples were regularly used to show committee members and others the accuracy of the manufacturers' details before an entire order was manufactured and shipped to the site.

As work moved toward the finishing stages, columns and their capitals soared above the Dome Room floor. Cornices and balustrades were now set, but the dome still showed bare tile (fig. 43).

Frames for the acoustical panels to line the dome spread like a giant spiderweb (fig. 44). The frames were attached to the tile and, in turn, supported sound-absorbing panels of plastic-coated aluminum backed with fiberglass. These panels may be removed for cleaning or for replacement if damaged.

41. Assembly of prefabricated balustrades atop entablature in Dome Room, June 1975.

42. Sample of stair trim, placed for inspection before
the entire order is cut at the mill, June 1975.

43. Column capitals in the dome room were cast from molding plaster to duplicate the designs Jefferson had originally provided in wood.

(R. E. Lee & Son, Inc., Report to Associated General Contractors of America, January 1977, p. 12. Photo taken July 1975.)

Finally, the scaffolds were ready to be moved for the last time in October 1975. The aluminum acoustical liner was in place (fig. 45).

Ballou conferred frequently with Nichols, with the chairman of the building committee, and with Construction Superintendent Fred Warner as the work progressed. Figure 46 shows him conferring with Warner (right), while Schuyler Reed, associate construction superintendent, checks a detail of construction in the background. Occasionally, changes had to be made on the spot as the result of a new discovery.

As noted earlier, the color of the roof raised questions and controversies and gave occasional moments of humor. Some committee members wanted the soft green of Stanford White's roof to be used again. To settle the question, the architect arranged a display of suggested colors, somewhat to the astonishment of passersby (fig. 47). The committee decided on white because it was attractive from a distance and had most likely been Jefferson's choice, since he had purchased only white paint for the university buildings while the Rotunda was under construction.

As mentioned above, finding the right wood for flooring is always expensive in restoration projects, but Mr. Power generously made heart pine of Jefferson's period available to the builders for a modest price. The wood was remanufactured from carefully selected boards. Figure 48 shows the flooring of different widths being laid over a cement base that gives fire protection, sound insulation, and firm support. Attention to details was necessary to conserve the supply of this precious wood.

Two-by-four "sleepers" were nailed to the poured concrete over steel joists. Voids were filled with sound-

119

44. Supports for the acoustical ceiling in the Dome
Room spread like a giant spiderweb, September 1975.

45. The acoustical liner inside the dome is aluminum
framed with a backing of two inches of rock wool.
Its surface is perforated aluminum, covered with
plastic fabric. (October 1975.)

46. Louis W. Ballou, architect (left), instructs Fred
Warner, construction superintendent, while Schuyler
Reed, associate construction superintendent, checks
a detail in the background, October 1975.

122

47. The harlequin Rotunda, as paint samples were applied in an effort to select the color for the dome, September 1975.

49. Old pine, remanufactured for flooring, is matched for color and grain before being laid, November 1975.

48. Workmen install subfloor, June 1975.

deadening insulation and a continuous plywood subfloor was nailed to the sleepers. The finished floor was then nailed to the sleepers. (See fig. 49.) This effort helped deaden sound in the Dome Room.

With the floor laid, samples of stain and varnish were applied in a selected area to determine their effects on the wood under the lighting conditions in the Dome Room (fig. 50). The committee made its decision, again proving that it could make good decisions amicably once all the facts had been made available. Vigorous discussions were common, reported Bice, but never hard feelings or intransigence.

The free-form stairs required close attention to detail. Said to be the first double free-standing stairs in the United States, they are of special interest to architects and builders. Framed over steel, the wooden stairs follow smooth curves along the walls of the oval rooms until they intersect with the exterior walls. There they turn along another set of curves (fig. 51).

Floors and stairs were now installed and finished, and the main hall neared completion. Rich tones of the floors, the stairs, and the walnut banister were apparent (fig. 52). Especially noticeable is the curved black-walnut handrail for the stairs (fig. 53). It receives its finish from the oil on the hands of people as they go up and down to the Dome Room. A master craftsman was brought from New York to fit all the parts of the rail together.

Finally, the Dome Room was completed, and it is breathtaking. One might say it sparkles.

The floors of old pine—richly stained, coated with polyurethane for finish and wear characteristics, and

50. Samples of stains applied, to aid in final selection, February 1976.

51. Curved stairs with fireplace in the free-form center hall, October 1975.

newly buffed—contrast sharply with the dark, dull surfaces seen during construction.

Indirect lighting on the balcony illuminates both the dome and the mezzanine. Light from the windows heightens the effect. Window lines are interrupted by a small circular stairway and fireplaces. The building contains Jefferson's eight original fireplaces: two in the Dome Room, one each in the three oval rooms on the main floor and in the east and west oval rooms in the basement, plus the one on the intermediate landing of the east stair to the Dome Room.

Being more specific about the details, Bobby Lee commented: "The finishes are unique. There is not a straight wall in any major space. From the installation of curved plaster grounds, through lathing, plastering, run plaster molding, applied ornamentation, unsymmetrical splayed paneled window jambs, paneled doors, curved wood stairways and balustrades, we [the contractors] demanded skills that had not been used in thirty years." (R. E. Lee to O. A. Gianniny, Jr., December 13, 1976.) (See figs. 54 and 55.)

To those who had literally spent years of their lives planning and hoping for the restoration, the moment of completion was overwhelming; there the Rotunda was, just as Jefferson had conceived and built it (fig. 56).

52. Center hall and stairs near completion, March 1976.

53. Completed curved stair and balustrade, November 1976.

54. and 55. Completed Dome Room, March 1976.

56. Completed Rotunda, over Homer's statue, December 1976.

Dedication

Dedication ceremonies were held on April 13, 1976, the 233rd anniversary of Thomas Jefferson's birth. This was one of the major events celebrating the bicentennial of the Declaration of Independence. In a simple service on the south portico, the architect, Louis W. Ballou, and the contractors, R. E. Lee and J. A. Kessler, Jr., presented the building to Mr. William F. Zimmer, rector of the University of Virginia. He, in turn, delivered the keys and documents to Dr. Frank L. Hereford, Jr. president. Behind Zimmer in figure 57 is Professor Emeritus B. F. D. Runk, bicentennial director for the university. Seated on the far left is former President Edgar F. Shannon, Jr., under whose guidance most of the restoration took place. Governor Mills E. Godwin, himself an alumnus, addressed the crowd assembled on the Lawn under a brilliant sky that mild spring afternoon.

That the Monticello Guard, local company of the National Guard, should have been present on this occasion is most appropriate because of its close associa-

57. Dedication ceremony, south portico, April 13, 1976. Front row: J. A. Kessler, R. E. "Bobby" Lee, Louis W. Ballou, William F. Zimmer, Frank L. Hereford, Jr. Second row: left, Edgar F. Shannon, Jr.; center, B. F. D. Runk.

tion with the University of Virginia since the guard unit was so named in 1857.[2] (See fig. 58.)

Figures 59 and 60—providing a panoramic view of the crowd attending the dedication—might be titled, "Were You There?" For years to come, these photographs will be enjoyed as a memento by those present on one of the great days of the university.

But the dedication was more than a ceremony; it was a series of actions and events that returned the Rotunda to the center of university life. Though early planners of the restoration had envisioned the building as housing the administrative offices of the president, Hereford decided against moving the offices to the Rotunda, thus releasing space for more varied activities.

The first major event, which took place in the Dome Room, was a premier exhibit in America of scale models of Palladio's buildings. Professor Nichols arranged with the Italian government to have the showing to celebrate the opening of the Rotunda. The exhibit was lent from Vicenza, and transportation was donated by Italy as a gift for the bicentennial. In this setting, the exhibit demonstrated the strong influence Palladio had had on Jefferson's design of the university. (See fig. 61.) Later the models were displayed in major museums throughout the country.

A second major event was the visit of Queen Elizabeth II of England, who was guest of honor at a luncheon in the Dome Room on July 10, 1976. This visit by Her Majesty was part of her tour celebrating what the British press called the "Bicentenary of the War for American Independence." President Hereford and other

---

2. See Robert Culin, *A Sketch of the History and Activities of the Monticello National Guard* (Charlottesville: Michie Publishing Co., 1939).

58. Monticello Guard serve as honor guard for the
dedication ceremony, April 13, 1976.

university officials were hosts in this expression of goodwill between the United States and Great Britain (fig. 62).

During the first two years following its completion, the restored Rotunda attracted from 800 to 1000 visitors per day, as touring Americans came to see Jefferson's last monumental building. Other uses also increased. Receptions and special academic events have been scheduled in the Dome Room. Students find it a quiet, congenial place for study. On the main floor, the Board of Visitors meets regularly in the east oval room. Doctoral examining committees and small groups use the north oval room. The west oval room housed the bicentennial office for the university for the first year, and is now the President's ceremonial office. In the basement, the oval rooms house the University Guide Service and a museum of university artifacts. The Admissions Office holds regular meetings with prospective students and their families in the west oval room. In the basement wings are the offices of the Vice-Presidents for Academic Affairs, for Student Affairs, for Finance, and for Development.

Two years after the dedication ceremony, the building was once again the symbolic center of the Academical Village. It reveals the architectural genius of Thomas Jefferson as well as the intervening history of the university. The large brick terrace north of the building is a remnant of the Annex. The north portico and the completed wings and courts, added by Stanford White, provide balance and acknowledge growth. As the university has grown and spread to become a small metropolis, the Lawn retains the symbolic "village" character, with the Rotunda restored to its central and meaningful place (fig. 63).

59. and 60. Audience at dedication ceremony, April 1976.

61. Palladio in America exhibit in completed Rotunda,
April 1976.

62. Queen Elizabeth II and President Frank L. Hereford, Jr., walk from Cabell Hall towards the Rotunda during the royal visit celebrating the bicentennial of the American Declaration of Independence, July 10, 1976. Governor Mills E. Godwin and Mrs. Ann Hereford appear in right background.

63. Looking south toward Cabell Hall from the Rotunda portico, October 1976.

The restored Rotunda has attracted visitors of many kinds from all sections of the country. The alumni of the class of 1926—who had come to be inducted into the Thomas Jefferson Society of Alumni, which honors graduates of fifty years or more—were fortunate to have Professor Vincent Shea as their guide on a special tour (fig. 64). Shea was an active member of the Rotunda Restoration Committee as well as the university's Vice-President for Business and Finance.

The University Guide Service has been interested from the very beginning in the restoration and use of the Rotunda. Each day during the summer and fall of 1976, they escorted visitors through the building. Figures 65, 66, and 67 show tour groups in the east oval room, basement level; the west oval room, basement level; and the center hall on the main floor, where the famous Galt statue of Thomas Jefferson now stands. Alumni like to tell how this massive marble piece, estimated to weigh 2000 lbs., was brought down from the Dome Room through the flame and smoke of the 1895 fire with hardly a scratch.

The oval room to the right of the main hall is the meeting place of the Board of Visitors, the governing body of the university. It is furnished with a large oval mahogany table made by Valley Crafters of Harrisonburg, Virginia, and a rug woven in India especially for this oval space (fig. 68). Over the mantel is a portrait of Dr. Edwin A. Alderman, first president of the University of Virginia from 1904 to 1931 (fig. 69).

Across the hall on the left is the president's ceremonial office, where distinguished visitors are met and where occasions of special significance are held. It is distinguished by a Sully portrait of Jefferson done when he was seventy (fig. 70).

64. The class of 1926 visits the restored Rotunda during their fiftieth reunion, April 1976. Vincent Shea, vice-president for business and finance served as guide.

During the last year of restoration work, students had raised questions about the use of the Rotunda; but since its reopening, Bice has stated that "more and more students are studying in the Rotunda. We bought ten very nice tables, one for each alcove, and we put four chairs around each. They are used almost all the time. We think its use is excellent"[3] (see figs. 71 and 72).

The view from the Dome Room looking down the Lawn is said to have been one of Jefferson's favorites as he watched the construction of his university (fig. 73). He once proposed that this window be replaced with a French door to give a better view of the distant mountains, but the window was retained. On one occasion Dr. Alderman remarked, concerning the Lawn, "The presence of Jefferson is so real here that one would not be surprised to meet him upon turning the next corner."[4]

The two busts (figs. 74 and 75) that face each other in the small oval room to the north on the main floor remind us that those two close friends Jefferson and Lafayette met here on the occasion of the first great public dinner at the still unfinished Rotunda on November 15, 1824. At that time Jefferson proposed the following in reply to Lafayette's toast: "If I could see it [the university] once enjoying the patronage and cherishment of our public authorities with undivided voice, I should die without a doubt of the future of my native state, and in the consoling contemplation of the happy influence of this institution on its character, its virtue, its prosperity, its safety."[5]

3. Personal interview with the authors, April 18, 1978.
4. *New York Times Magazine*, Sunday, April 12, 1925, p. 2, col. 1.
5. Quoted in Bruce, *History of the University of Virginia, 1819–1919*, 2:331.

65. University Guide Service conducts tours of the university, starting from the restored Rotunda, October 1976.

66. Office of Admissions holds regular meetings for prospective students and parents in the Rotunda, June 1977.

67. Visitors admire the great free-form hall and oval rooms on the main floor, October 1976.

68. In the east oval room, where the Board of Visitors
meets, a large mahogany table, chandeliers, and an
oval rug handwoven in India give gracious atmosphere,
October 1976.

69. A portrait of Edwin A. Alderman, first president of the university, hangs in the east oval room, main floor, October 1976.

70. West oval room, main floor was used as the bicentennial office, October 1976. Sully portrait of Jefferson hangs over the mantel.

71. *and* 72. Students study in the restored Dome Room
alcoves, October 1976.

73. Cabell Hall and students on the Lawn, through Jefferson's favorite window in the Dome Room, October 1976.

74. and 75. Busts of Jefferson and Lafayette in the north oval room, main floor, October 1976.

153

The Father of the University would have been glad to hear Governor Mills E. Godwin affirm in his dedication address at the Rotunda on April 13, 1976: "Virginia takes great pride in this University, and it is fitting that today, its Founder's birthday, we should dedicate this Rotunda which stands at its very heart."[6]

A final tribute was paid by George Rodrigue, a student, in the *Cavalier Daily*, April 13, 1976:

> *The Rotunda has been burned, dynamited, shot at, and bled upon. It has been stuffed with books, jammed full of students, gutted twice and restored three times since Mr. Jefferson's plans for "something of the grand kind" as a centerpiece of his academical village were translated into brick and mortar in the spring of 1823.*
>
> *Through reconstruction, renovation, and adaptation, however, the building has remained the spiritual and architectural focal point of the University. The Jeffersonian ideal of a synthesis between beauty and functionality was, and some say, still is, the guiding light for construction of the entire University and especially the Rotunda.*

6. Quoted in *Charlottesville Daily Progress*, April 14, 1976, p. 1.

76. Oculus in the Dome Room, October 1976.

Appendix A
Chronology of Restoration and Adaptation
(according to contractor's work schedule)

9/1/73–10/1/73	Erection of temporary construction facilities
10/1/73–1/20/74	Interior demolition
1/21/74–3/1/74	Excavation and underpinning
2/10/74–5/1/74	Concrete work at ground floor
5/1/74–7/15/74	First-floor concrete, framing, and masonry
7/15/74–11/1/74	Dome Room and balconies: framing and concrete
4/1/74–12/1/74	Roofing and sheet-metal removal, concrete work, and installation of dome stepped rings and skylight
7/1/74–12/1/74	Masonry chimneys, spiral stairs, and elevator-shaft preparation
11/1/74–6/1/75	Lath and plaster, ceramic and marble work, brick floors
5/1/74–2/1/76	Mechanical, plumbing, sprinkler, and electrical systems
5/1/75–11/15/75	Carpentry finished
8/1/75–12/15/75	Flooring finished
12/1/75–1/1/76	Painted interior and installed finished trim
11/1/75–2/1/76	Removal of temporary construction facilities

NOTE: All work was actually completed in time for dedication of the building on April 13, 1976.

Appendix B
Principal Participants in Restoration and Adaptation
RESTORATION COMMITTEE

Appointed on September 21, 1965, by President Edgar
F. Shannon, Jr.

Francis L. Berkeley, Jr., chairman
Dumas Malone
Bernard Mayo
Charles Smith
William Zuk
Werner K. Sensbach, ex officio
Vincent Shea, ex officio
Edgar F. Shannon, Jr., ex officio
Frederick D. Nichols, ex officio

Others who joined the committee in 1965–66

Roy Eugene Graham
Matthias E. Kayhoe (1965–66)

Appointments as revised by President-elect Frank L. Hereford, Jr.,
on August 29, 1974.

Raymond C. Bice, chairman
Dumas Malone
Frederick D. Nichols
Vincent Shea
Werner K. Sensbach
William Zuk
Avery Catlin
Frank L. Hereford, Jr., ex officio

ARCHITECTS

The firm of Ballou and Justice of Richmond, Virginia, was appointed
architects on April 2, 1966.

Frederick D. Nichols was appointed architectural research consultant
by the architects in 1966. He had also been appointed in 1952 as
architect for restoration of the Jefferson buildings of the university.

CONTRACTOR

R. E. Lee & Son, Inc., of Charlottesville, was awarded the contract
for restoration and adaptation in July 1973.

Appendix C
Photographers' Notes

This brief essay summarizes the procedures used by the photographers, during construction, to obtain the record on color slides and, following construction, to verify the validity of the record through review by interested parties. As stated above, the photographers were laymen, with respect to decisions, design, and construction in this project, and they have attempted to remain true to that point of view. Many persons assisted in getting the coverage, as acknowledged elsewhere in this book.

The 1973–76 photographic records of restoration were kept by many persons. The architect, the contractor, the University Information Service, the university Office of Planning, *the Cavalier Daily*, the *Charlottesville Daily Progress*, and others made some photographic records. Our own collection contains approximately 2000 color slides showing all phases of the work, including some before and after images.

The record was kept regularly, usually on a weekly basis. One or the other of us usually photographed the work site on Thursday afternoons, beginning at about 2:00 P.M. Additional visits were made when the contractor or architect advised us of particularly interesting activities or discoveries. As a result, we believe this record to be the most comprehensive photographic account of the work as it progressed. Furthermore, the use of color gave a dimension of detail we would have been unable to capture otherwise, for both aesthetic and documentary purposes.

On a few occasions when neither of us could be present, our capable and gracious faculty colleague Luther Yates Gore, associate professor and former chairman of the Division of Humanities, maintained the continuity of the record. His photographs are imaginative and well done. Frequently they suggested alternative approaches we had not previously used.

Throughout the construction period, we maintained our individual styles and photographic interests, agreeing to cover essentials but that each would convey the spirit of the project as he felt it. Thus, we experimented with ways to photograph the work in progress. There were enough technical problems in photographing to satisfy fully our interests in that direction. Given the low levels of available light, the low levels of reflectivity of many construction materials, and the distances involved for indoor shooting, we were frequently discovering the limits of our equipment and skill.

A summary of our photographic equipment will indicate something of the limitations. Our flash equipment was usually a Vivitar 271 automatic electronic flash unit, designed for a "hot-shoe" mount atop the camera. The guide number for this flash unit is 110 for film speed of ASA 160 in manual operation, with a light delivery of 1400 beam candlepower seconds, at a 60° horizontal and 50° vertical angle of illumination. The flash unit is designed for use at distances of 10–15 feet, with 50-mm lenses; for our purposes dark walls had to be illuminated at a distance of 50 feet or more, with a 28-mm lens.

In the early stages, our cameras were a Mamiya/Sekor DTL 1000 and a Pentax Spotmatic II. Both served well, but neither is considered a top-of-the-line professional camera. Lenses were either Takumar, made for the Pentax, or Vivitar, a universal lens that would fit either camera body. We resorted to 28 mm (though a few were taken with a 24 mm) focal length for wide-angle shots and to a telephoto lens, usually a 135 mm. Some pictures were made using a zoom lens: initially a Vivitar 85–205 mm, with f/3.5 maximum aperture.

Later, in 1975 and 1976, the Mamiya/Sekor camera was replaced by a second Pentax Spotmatic II, and the original Pentax with a Nikkormat. Fixed focal-length lenses were then all Takumar or Nikkor, and the zoom lens was replaced with a Vivitar "Series One" Macrozoom, with a range of focal lengths of 70–210 mm and a maximum aperture of f/3.5.

Early in the project, our film was Kodak Ektachrome, ASA 160, balanced for daylight—the fastest reliable Kodak film available at the time. It was processed by Kodak, using their E-4 process. When interior surfaces become bright and more highly reflective, we used Kodachrome X film, at a film speed of ASA 64. This too was processed by Kodak. In 1975, a new family of Kodachrome films became available, and from that time on, whenever light conditions permitted, we used Kodachrome 64, ASA 64, again with Kodak processing.

Slides were processed as soon as they were exposed and were reviewed as soon as they were returned. In most instances, they were labeled individually for future identification. If the pictures were faulty, we usually attempted to shoot them again, correcting the fault. We duplicated many shots, exposing at different light levels ("bracketing") when light level readings were unreliable. When supplementary light meters were needed, we used a Luna-Pro meter with cadmium sulfide batteries and a 7 1/2-degree-angle spot attachment.

A typical visit was preceded by a conference between us on Monday or Tuesday, when slides from the preceding week had been returned. A critique of those slides and an anticipated coverage plan was worked out. We had access to the contractor's work schedule, so we consulted it to learn what would be interesting that week. On Thursday afternoon, the photographer for that week (on a few occasions, both photographers) went to the office of the construction superintendent, where he donned a bright-orange safety helmet and checked on the special activities of the day.

If one of the construction superintendents was in the office, he would describe special activities. Sometimes one of the foremen would be present, perhaps in conference over details. He would also offer suggestions for interesting coverage. Then too, eventually the regular employees at the work site got to know us—greeting us, or referring to us as "the little fat man" or "the other guy, with the beard"—and they would have ideas for shots as well.

We had free access to work areas, subject only to the same safety rules as the workmen, so the only limitations were those of our equipment, imagination, and safety. To avoid undue hazards, we carried a minimal amount of equipment; shoulder gadget bags—containing such equipment as lenses, film, and spare batteries, and perhaps a notebook—were the only extras. All photographs were taken with hand-held cameras often steadied against firm structures when the shutter speed was very low.

After touring the job site, we often reviewed what we had seen with Fred Warner, construction superintendent, who sometimes had further suggestions and always provided some background for what we had seen. During each tour we may well have seen at least one of the principal parties to the restoration: Ballou, Lee, Kessler, Nichols, or Bice.

As the work neared completion, we felt a need for some review of our slides to confirm our sense of the work and to give technical linkages between the images and the understandings that led to the work. We felt the need to connect our work to that of the contractor as a possible aid to future scholars of the restoration. Fred Warner volunteered to review our slides and to comment on them in tape-recorded statements. We started him with a few, but his enthusiasm led him to comment on about 1500. These comments are preserved on magnetic tape and are indexed to particular trays of slides. We are indebted to him for his time, energy, and knowledge of detail.

From time to time, Ballou visited Joseph L. Vaughan as a personal friend, and during these visits he saw enough of the slides to assure himself, and us, that our approach was sound.

Initially we had planned to close out the effort after construction was complete and the building was dedicated, and on April 13, 1976, we had completed the construction slides and Warner's commentaries.

During the summer, we prepared a system for cataloging the slides for future use and began to think about their possible public use. For example, several members of the construction crew asked when they might see them. Some even suggested that we show them after work some day with appropriate refreshments, but others suggested an evening showing so their families could see what they had been doing. These men were proud of their part in this historic restoration and wanted their names associated with the work.

The University of Virginia Alumni Association indicated interest in using the slides to inform those who had not yet visited the new Rotunda what they could expect. In response to this request, and bearing in mind the interest of the workers, we prepared a slide show using two simultaneous images (sometimes called "paired image" presentation) with about 180 slides and live commentary. This show was presented first to a small group of twelve interested persons who would give it a critical review, representing alumni, university, community, and families. This presentation was given in the board room of Alumni Hall on October 3, 1976. Our critics enjoyed what they saw and encouraged us to complete the presentation by including pictures of the now-completed Rotunda in use. Following their suggestion, we returned once again, cameras in hand, almost six months to the day after the dedication ceremony.

Our expanded presentation consisted of 240 slides and was also arranged for a paired-image showing and live commentary, lasting 30–35 minutes. This version of the slide collection was first shown in the Rotunda for the Albemarle Art Association on December 11, 1976. Approximately seventy-five persons attended, and following the showing, they toured the building with James Ee. Kinard, curator of the Rotunda. This showing initiated a new phase of our work, that of adapting the material for different audiences.

Our second mode of presentation was a report prepared for use by R. E. Lee & Son, Inc., in application for a "Build America" award from the Associated General Contractors of America (AGC)/Motorola. That presentation grew out of the Rotunda showing, described above, at which R. E. Lee approached Allan Gianniny about using some of our slides for his report as he thought our slides superior to the photographic record kept by his company. We agreed to help Mr. Lee and met with him two days later. At that time we accepted his invitation to serve as consultants to his company to write a narrative account of the restoration, to select appropriate photographs from our collection, to supervise their printing, and to lay out the report.

The report was due January 15, 1977, so for the next four weeks we followed a rigorous schedule in its preparation. Lee, J. A. Kessler, Jr., president, and R. E. "Robin" Lee, Jr., treasurer, assisted us in perfecting the text and emphasis within the report. R. E. Lee also reviewed many of the slides in our collection, offering his comments on their importance, both singly and as a collection. With the help given by all these gentlemen, plus that of others in the company, the report—accompanied by specifications, drawings, and related testimonial letters—was submitted to AGC on time. In late February, the company received word that they had won the award, and R. E. Lee went to San Francisco to accept the award for his company. Three copies of our report were prepared: one for AGC, one for R. E. Lee & Son, Inc., and one that we retained.

Several showings of the slides followed during the spring of 1977—most sponsored by the University Guide Service, who had been interested in the first showing to the Art Association. One of the showings was presented for the university and local community in South Meeting Room, Newcomb Hall, on April 12, 1977, as part of the Jefferson's birthday celebration. Other showings were held for the purpose of training guides. Nichols used sixty-one slides in an illustrated lecture for architecture students. Ballou used ten in a report to HUD. Lee had used ten in a presentation to AGC in San Francisco, and another fifty appeared in the report described above.

Commencing on April 13, 1977, Newcomb Hall Gallery showed thirty-five 11×14 prints made by Allan Gianniny from the slides. This exhibit continued until June 10.

The paired-image show was given before the Faculty Wives' Club of the university on November 11, 1977, in the Rotunda, with approximately ninety persons attending.

In the spring of 1978, an abbreviated slide and tape show was prepared for the Alumni Association for automated showing at meetings away from the university.

In the meantime, the decision had been made to prepare the present book for general audiences after supplementing our original work with a series of interviews with the principal participants in the project. During the spring of 1978, we interviewed Ballou, Nichols, Bice, and Berkeley; in October 1978, Kessler; and in June 1979, Shannon. Unfortunately, R. E. Lee died as the result of an accident, so we are dependent on the earlier materials for his views.

From this account, the reader might properly glean the idea that we are still learning about the restoration, for the search leads to other interesting questions: especially concerning the historic background and the concepts that have been intimately associated with this building.

On Jefferson's concepts of the Rotunda and the original university, the best sources available in print, and the most authoritative, are the following.

Frederick D. Nichols, *Thomas Jefferson's Architectural Drawings*, compiled with commentary and checklist. Boston: Massachusetts Historical Society; Charlottesville, Va.: Thomas Jefferson Memorial Society and University of Virginia Press, 1961.

 Professor Nichols's collection includes Jefferson's drawings for the university and for his other major buildings. Nichols's checklist has become the standard for cataloging Jefferson drawings in Alderman Library's Manuscript Division.

William B. O'Neal, *Jefferson's Buildings at the University of Virginia: The Rotunda*. Charlottesville, Va.: The University of Virginia Press, 1960.

 Professor O'Neal traces the conception and construction of the original Rotunda in an essay including excerpts from the correspondence of Jefferson and his colleagues engaged in planning and building, from 1817 until the building was substantially complete in October 1828. His plates show both the Rotunda and the major reference plates from Palladio, used by Jefferson. It is an attractive book, as well as a useful one.

 For a history of the Rotunda from its construction until the great fire of 1895, an excellent source is Frederick D. Nichols, "Phoenix in Virginia" (*Arts in Virginia* 1, no. 3, [Spring 1961]: 23–29). Jefferson drawings and photographs from the prefire era illustrate the article.

 An interesting collection of articles about the fire and its aftermath, including the work of rebuilding the university in the period from 1895 until 1900, appears in quarterly issues of the *Alumni Bulletin of the University of Virginia*. This journal, initiated in May 1894, was an official publication of the faculty, carrying news and extended accounts of developments at the university. After the fire, the journal published reports of eyewitnesses and of efforts to raise funds and to select architects. Excerpts from the first report by McKim, Mead & White were published, as were detailed articles by Professor Francis H. Smith (November 1895) and William Mynn Thornton, chairman of the faculty. The November 1895 issue appeared sometime after March 1896, so it contained much reaction to the fire. It also published the rendering Stanford White offered of his new design. In 1898, the August issue was entitled "Restoration Issue." Minor articles on the rebuilding of the university continued to appear in the *Bulletin* well into the first decade of the twentieth century.

A history of the Rotunda also appears in *Philip Alexander Bruce, History of the University of Virginia, 1819–1919* (5 vols.; New York: Macmillan, 1921). Volume 1 contains sections on the original design of the university, and volume 2 describes its opening years. Volume 4 describes the fire and its aftermath and the reconstruction. Bruce speculates that Jefferson might have preferred a scheme like White's. As is often the case throughout all five volumes, however, he gives no source for his speculation.

Newspapers in Charlottesville and Richmond carried a number of articles during and after the reconstruction, many of which may be found in the vertical files of Alderman Library.

There is no comprehensive history of the Stanford White version of the Rotunda, the version in existence during essentially half the life-span of the university.

Articles related to the restoration of Jefferson's original design began to appear in local newspapers in the early 1960s. The *Cavalier Daily* and the *Charlottesville Daily Progress* began to follow the new interest in this endeavor led by Professor Nichols and his colleagues and by Professor Francis L. Berkeley, Jr. Other new newspapers in Charlottesville and in the university, such as the *Jefferson Journal* and the *Declaration* published articles on the restoration of the Rotunda. Student newspapers ran regular accounts of controversies over use of the building. The vertical files in Alderman Library contain a collection of many of these articles.

The *Alumni News* carried two articles that are informative and interesting. The July-August issue of 1972 carried a definitive article by Professor Berkeley describing the planning and the projected uses of the building. The January-February issue of 1976 carried a readable and useful article by Elizabeth Wilkerson on the construction work to that time.

Photographs of the work in progress appeared in the *Alumni News*, the *Cavalier Daily*, the *Charlottesville Daily Progress*, and the *Richmond Times-Dispatch* at frequent, though irregular, intervals.

Copies of the architect's drawings and specifications are held by the architect, the contractor, and the university. Field drawings and subcontractor's documents are held by the contractor, as is his work schedule and his diary of the construction.

Illustration Credits

Frontispiece; fig. opposite Part II (Nichols models of the Rotunda); and figs, 13, 15, 16, 17, 18–19, 20, 21, 22, 23, 24, 25, 26, 27, 28, 29, 30, 31, 32, 33, 34, 35, 36, 37, 38, 39, 40, 41, 42, 43, 44, 45, 46, 47, 48, 49, 50, 51, 52, 53, 54, 55, 56, 57, 58, 59, 60, 61, 63, 64, 65, 66, 67, 68, 69, 70, 71, 72, 73, 74, 75, 76: Joseph L. Vaughan and O. Allan Gianniny, Jr.

Fig. opposite Introduction (Rotunda book plate, ca. 1827): Rare Book Department, University of Virginia Library

Figs. 1, 2, 3, 4: Thomas Jefferson Architectural Drawings (Nichols 328, 329, 330, 331), Manuscripts Department, University of Virginia Library

Fig. 5: Paul Brandon Barringer, James Mercer Garnett, and Rosewell Page, eds., *University of Virginia: Its History, Influence, Equipment, and Characteristics* (New York: Lewis Publishing Co., 1904), p. 48.

Fig. 6 and fig. opposite Part I ("University . . . from the East"): Betts Collection (nos. 9, 47), Manuscripts Department, University of Virginia Library

Fig. 7: University of Virginia Archives (RG-5/7/2.762), Manuscripts Department, University of Virginia Library

Fig. 8: Edward R. Stettinius Papers (accession no. 2723), Manuscripts Department, University of Virginia Library

Fig. 9: McDonald Bros. Collection (accession no. 8918), Manuscripts Department, University of Virginia Library

Fig. 10: McKim, Mead and White Collection (accession no. 1414-b), Manuscripts Department, University of Virginia Library

Fig. 11: Holsinger Collection (no. U-302-B), Manuscripts Department, University of Virginia Library

Fig. 12: Printing Services, Photographic Division, University of Virginia

Fig. 14: Kenneth Brown collection, courtesy of Jerry Showalter; photo by Joseph L. Vaughan and O. Allan Gianniny, Jr.

Fig. 62: Amir M. Pishad, photographer, Richmond Newspapers, Inc.

Index

Numbers in italics refer to illustrations.

Index